# THE MISCHIEVIOUS ATHALETE:

## THE POCKET BOOK OF (PROPER) ENGLISH PRONUNCIATION

# THE MISCHIEVIOUS ATHALETE:

## THE POCKET BOOK OF (PROPER) ENGLISH PRONUNCIATION

### WILLIAM CRITCHLEY

FIRST ENGLISH BOOKS

First Published in Great Britain in 2017 by First English Books

The right of William Critchley to be identified as the author of this work has been asserted by him in accordance with the Copyright, Designs and Patents Act, 1988.

ISBN-10: 0-9551437-8-0
ISBN-13: 978-0-9551437-8-6

Cover design/interior book design: Lisa DeSpain
Proofreading/index: Michèle Moody (was Clarke)

Printed and bound in Great Britain

*A CIP catalogue record for this book is available from the British Library.*

# CONTENTS

Preface........................................................................................ix

Introduction...................................................................................1
*The Queen and 'cawst' of ships – Demosthenes' trick – mockney –
the groompy and 'cloomsy' doock (duck) from St James' Park –
regional newsreaders – weather forecasters – good speakers of
English – discussions of some political figures – Tony Blair goes to
school etc. – Scouse accents, proud Liverpudlians – how to start a
controversy – notes on linguistics – pronunciation guides on the net –
phonetics and vowels – a poem to practise*

Chapter One...................................................................................27
*Ladies in Waitrose buying scōnes – 'Ma'am' rhymes with jam – a
'weasel' with words – cold grouse and a good claret for breakfast –
'Must get in me* [sic] *car' – Chilcot report – acting school*

Chapter Two...................................................................................33
*Care needed when addressing people – black spider memos –
how to write a letter to a member of the Royal Family – Taff,
Jock and Ginger – Debrett's Peerage – two important words to
remember – confusion with accents – more presenters with regional
accents – clichés and stock phrases – goodbye to i.e., e.g. and etc. –
pronunciation of some letters and vowels – haitch – hypercorrection –
eye-ther or ee-ther, US pronunciations – some English 'howlers' – a
few bêtes noires – counterintuitive pronunciations*

Chapter Three.................................................................................63
*Miss Annie Ting – an Irish yarn (poor old Fido) – Rick
Stein's pistachios – Victor Meldrew's gooseberries – more odd or
different pronunciations – Kingsley Amis sounds off – guns over
Kimmeridge Bay*

Chapter Four .......................................................................... 71

*This 'correction malarkey' – my friend gets 'mizled' – more difficult words for non-native speakers – the wonder of everyday accents – Mr Eric Pickles MP on* Desert Island Discs *– Si qua est et gloria (If there is any glory in this...)*

Chapter Five .......................................................................... 77

*The dastardly perpetrators! Bring them to justice! Burglars and coupons – using déclassé in conversations – plumping for Occam's razor – words of four or more syllables – gender – some TV shows – crafting on TV – play Sudoku for ever!*

Chapter Six .......................................................................... 85

*More game and reality shows – Mrs May 'a big pointless pot of low-fat yoghurt' – Giles Coren to eat children 'if Jeremy Corbyn wins next election' – 'sticklers' à la David Starkey – dress rules for men – dialects – 'the fat, bald bloke on MasterChef' – some word meanings explained – David Dimbleby in Doncaster – long and short 'a's*

Chapter Seven .......................................................................... 103

*Difficult words to pronounce – some explanations – apocryphal story from Sir Nicholas Soames, grandson of Winston Churchill – 'slips of the tongue' in Parliament – gerrymander or gerrymonger*

Chapter Eight .......................................................................... 111

*Often or 'offen' – 'them' and 'those' – 'again' and 'agen' – rolling your 'r's – crafting and quilting – maxed out on toadstool fairies and 'amstas*

Chapter Nine .......................................................................... 119

*Times Diary (TMS) – apocryphal story about philosopher Bertrand Russell – three more tips (three words to make sure you say correctly) – accents in the UK – cod have 'regional accents' – female grime rappers – words in families – the importance of speech in human evolution*

Chapter Ten .......................................................................... 129

*Question tags – more on hypercorrection – the 'Home Counties' explained – a family history – Blackpool v the sunny south – Scottish independence and who owns all the grouse moors*

Chapter Eleven ........................................................ 137
*'Reet gradely' – extract from a poem by William Barnes – British*
*English (BrE) and American English (AmE) word differences –*
*Tooting Bec – when Kennedy was shot*

Chapter Twelve ....................................................... 143
*Received Pronunciation (RP) – Estuary English – CAT theory of*
*communication – John Betjeman – renowned phonetician John*
*Wells – girls and boys' names to avoid – some Irish, Scottish and*
*Welsh given names – Prince Charles and 'splendid' – 'hedgehog*
*super highway' using Joanna Lumley's Garden Bridge – Professor*
*Higgins and Eliza Doolittle meet at art gallery*

Postscript ............................................................. 155
*Inclusiveness – 'upspeak' (the high rising terminal) – a note on*
*alma maters – sounds of speech – some faux pas – Riesling or*
*Reisling – lunch or dinner? – U and non-U examples – the trap–*
*bath split – serendipity with words – more on dress codes for men –*
*a 'double' apocryphal story – more that unites us than divides –*
*'tongues are beautiful' – au revoir to the mischievious athalete*
*and the grumpy duck!*

Appendix 1 ........................................................... 175

Addenda .............................................................. 181

Glossary of Terms ................................................... 193

Notes and References ............................................... 211

Select Bibliography ................................................. 217

Index .................................................................. 219

For Kenneth Rowles

'Our language is funny – a "fat chance" and a
"slim chance" are the same thing.'
J. Gustav White

'Finis coronat opus.'
Anon.

# PREFACE

WILLIAM CRITCHLEY IS A writer and editor with over 30 years' experience in publishing. His alma maters were Canford School in Dorset and the Inns of Court School of Law. He was called to the Bar by the Middle Temple in 1980. Actually this is untrue; the Inns of Court School of Law wasn't exactly 'nourishing'; it was the Middle Temple that was the nourishing mother: the many dinners, the port, the gowns, royal portraits, the double hammerbeam roof, the 'Cup Board' – a table made from the hatch cover of the *Golden Hind*, the ship in which Drake sailed round the world – and Lord Denning mingling with the Benchers, and giving fine speeches. In those days there was even a lady who walked round, like cinema usherettes did in the interval, with a tray of lusciously fat cigars for sale. To clear one's head after the port and cigars, Fountain Court with its mulberry trees was the most agreeable place to pause awhile with the plashing water for company.

His other 'alma mater' was West Africa. Aged 18 he spent three months in West Cameroon as an assistant game warden, and then returned there aged 20, as the holder of a Winston Churchill Travelling Fellowship for Adventure and Exploration. He led a six-month expedition to study lowland gorillas in the Takamanda Forest Reserve, now a national park.

He now runs an online training course (LearnFree-lancing.com), and habitually annoys his three grown-up children by pointing out peculiarities in the English language. The most recent example was his younger son saying he had found a new pub called 'The Crown and Spectre'. Do you mean 'The Crown and Sceptre? You see, a sceptre is this magical symbol of sovereignty...A spectre is altogether less pleasant.'

It might take only a few milliseconds for him to come up with, 'Don't you know? Richard II..."This royal throne of kings, this sceptred isle...this other Eden, demi-para-dise...This precious stone set in a silver sea..."' 'Can you please be quiet, Dad?'

So he stayed quiet and wrote *The Mischievious Athalete: The Pocket Book of (Proper) English Pronunciation* instead.

*Note to Reader: Under each chapter heading is a list of topics and themes encountered in that chapter. The headings within chapters generally follow these introductory subheadings but not slavishly; so the general aim of the headings within each chapter is to guide the Reader to the main points in the book. Notes on pronunciation methods are also added from time to time in various chapters.*

# INTRODUCTION

*The Queen and 'cawst' of ships – Demosthenes' trick –
mockney –the groompy and 'cloomsy' doock (duck)
from St James' Park – regional newsreaders – weather
forecasters – good speakers of English – discussions of
some political figures – Tony Blair goes to school etc. –
Scouse accents, proud Liverpudlians – how to start
a controversy – notes on linguistics – pronunciation
guides on the net – phonetics and vowels – a poem
to practise*

WELL NOT SO MUCH 'posh' pronunciation as proper,
as in 'how to speak proper'! Like a great many
people, listening to TV and radio makes one realise how
modern speech has been abused. It's not *that* important;
being pedantic, judgemental or overcritical, especially
about regional accents is not the aim of this short book.
I hope it serves as a guide to younger people (and the
more mature), if only to help them avoid simple 'howlers',
including ordinary solecisms and peccadilloes, or trifling
faults. Perhaps it can also help readers to avoid minor
gaffes and embarrassments in conversation.

Of course everything changes in time. Gone are the silly, affected, and effete commentators of an earlier era. Even the Queen has had to adapt to changing times. Watching a black and white newsreel clip of Her Majesty about to launch a ship, I was amazed to hear her say that the vessel was ready to sail, despite, she said, the 'very considerable *cawst*'.

Presumably she felt it beneath her to pronounce the word as 'cost', in much the same way that old tea planters from India used to refer to game that had been hung too long as '*gawn awff*'. Much of the raison d'être for this short book was mainly tiresome newsreaders who often struggle with pronunciation. Yet, because there is still a department which advises on foreign words, or so I believe, you will find an English newsreader floundering with some English words but pronouncing foreign place names like polyglot linguists.

It's good to pronounce words right. Watch out for 'proNOUNCEi-ation' instead of proNUNciation! This catches quite a few people out. One pro*noun*ces the pro-*nun*ciation. Note also renounce and renunciation, where the 'nown' sound changes to 'nun'.

## Demosthenes' trick

Good pronunciation is also about 'enunciation' – speaking clearly and articulately. Elocution be damned! By this is meant 'elocution lessons', advised only in truly desperate straits. Lord Denning (alma mater: Magdalen College,

Oxford) spoke with a pronounced 'Hampshire bur' and was loved all the more for it. One might suggest Demosthenes (384–322 BC) as a good example. To develop his skills as an orator, Demosthenes put pebbles in his mouth to engender, or force, fluency in speech. He also recited verses while running, and spoke aloud by roaring waves on the Aegean seashore as a way of strengthening his oratory.

Please don't expect a treatise (treat-tĭs, not treat-īse) on linguistics here. It's much too difficult a subject for the simple wordsmith. As for grammar and punctuation, there are a few, but not many, passing mentions here. Consider it as more like 'the Zero Approach to Pronunciation' – not punctuation!

## Mockney

There's no escaping 'mockney' and lazy speech today. '*It's like, you know, more like, like too many people gettin' nuffink, like* [or *loike,* depending on region] *when they wan'ed sumfink, an' everyone else just ashoomed it was gonna be pisseasy.*' You can hear this kind of 'trash talk' any night of the week on numerous TV channels.

Mockney is a portmanteau word – two meanings in one word – mock and cockney. The *Urban Dictionary* defines it as: 'An upper class celebrity who attempts to solicit the admiration of the common person pretending to have a cockney accent', and in so doing sound like the ordinary man, and so gain some street cred or respect. (The latter is sometimes pronounced 'respeck' in 'Estuary English'.)

A solecism, by the way, is defined as 'the non-standard use of a grammatical construction; any mistake, incongruity, or absurdity; also a violation of good manners'. If you are one of those people who believes that 'everything happens for a reason', there is a nice reason behind the word. It's from the Greek, *soloikos*, speaking incorrectly. The original culprits came from *Soloi*, 'an Athenian colony of Cilicia where the inhabitants spoke a corrupt form of Greek'.[1]

If Latté (as in a coffee drink made with espresso and steamed milk), is it *Lahtay* or Lătee or even La'ee? Up north (and in many other parts of the country), no disrespect to northerners, the vowels come into contention – and not just the vowels. Take words like *con*tention or *con*vince or *con*sistent. Have you ever heard a northerner pronounce ONE correctly? It sounds 'right peculiar', a sort of top-heavy 'WHON'. (That's not to say they pronounce the '*wh*' like Americans or Scottish people do, as in 'He's having a *wwhhale* of a time.')

'One' should be sounded much more delicately. Some people do tend to come down heavily on the first syllable in words like *con*tention, *con*vince, *con*sistent. The stress is not on the first part of the word but (subtly) on the second part. You get the same errors with words like 'acknowledged'. It's made to sound like, 'He ACK-nowledged', which gives it an ugly sound, whereas the better form of pronunciation is to say, 'He ack*NOWL*edged' (to sound like ack*knoll*edged). *Note to reader: some parts of a word* *may be in capitals to show the stress intended but this is not consistently applied.*

Vowels (the way they are pronounced) can lead to all sorts of problems. Try saying 'Newcastle' with a long 'a' in Nucassel or Newcassel and you might get hurt. Geordies are tough. The difference is so great that I sometimes allow myself a flight of fancy with the words 'grumpy duck'.

Winston Churchill comes out of Parliament and almost trips over an angry mallard from St James' Park. He says in a fierce drawl to the bird, 'You grumpy duck'.

## The grumpy/clumsy duck makes its first appearance

Either of the Chuckle (*Chookle?*) Brothers comes out of St James' Park on the way to the Strangers Gallery in Parliament and almost trips over a cross duck. He says, '*You groompy doock*' but, instead of sounding right, it sounds (to a southerner) ridiculous, so much so that if you say it quietly to yourself you begin to laugh, and imagine the music hall must be just around the corner. (I'm sorry to say when I hear 'the bookies' [bukkies] pronounced as 'the booookies', I get the same feeling.)

Imagine you're in a middle-class bar ('we're all middle class now') in Nucassel and you bump into Lord Prescott (alma mater: Ruskin College and University of Hull). I don't really know why in Newcastle because he was born in Wales, and is very proud of being Welsh. (John Prescott when in the Merchant Navy as a steward became a left-wing union activist. On board one ship was Sir Anthony Eden enjoying a cruise; Prescott also won several boxing bouts at sea, which accounts for his famous 'punch' years later.) You tread (for the sake of the argument) on his left foot, and he says crossly, 'You're a clumsy duck, pal.' Now if he called me a CLUMSY DUCK, I expect I'd feel embarrassed but if it came out as 'CLOOMSY DOOCK', I don't think I could take it quite so seriously, even though he might be foaming at the mouth. So tiny little variations or fluctuations in vowel sounds are as noticeable today as they always were, even though the preponderance of regional newsreaders on the BBC would like you to think otherwise.

## Regional newsreaders

The question of Scottish newsreaders perplexed me for some time. I'm sure it I went to Scotland, I would'na hear English newsreaders to quite the same extent.

With its left-wing bias, BBC apparatchiks can happily employ a Scots person because they will be sure to get all the short vowels in, and deflect anyone away from noticing in a cloud of oat dust [*pace* (pronounced par-kay, 'with respect to') the great Dr Johnson in *Dictionary of the English Language*: '*Oats*. A grain, which in England is generally given to horses, but in Scotland supports the people.'] This was confirmed by a recent *Times* article.[2]

A new poll of radio listeners found that 'the nation's favourite radio voices have Scottish, Welsh and Jamaican

(Neil Nunes) accents'. But why should this be? The answer was that 'English people respond well to regional accents because the speaker's social class is not immediately clear.' Eddie Mair was very popular along with Susan Rae (both Scottish). Niall Paterson is yet another Scot on Sky News, John Humphrys heads up the Welsh contingent along with Huw Edwards. Kirsty Young, another Scot, is reported as saying (re accents beyond London and the southeast) that: 'It's a fashion. There's also the classless thing – to an Irish or Scottish person, that voice has class, and you can place it, but to most English people they can't place an Irish or Scottish accent in class terms.'[3] So that's why you'll find so many Scottish and Irish accents (Eamonn Holmes, the late Sir Terry Wogan) on TV too – because English people can listen or watch without having to bother to form an accurate class judgement! Glenn Campbell (BBC) is another Scot, as is Iain Watson, as is Gavin Esler. He's pretty good on the whole, but likes to drop in some 'short vowels' from time to time. ITV incidentally has many excellent newsreaders too.

Through the night on BBC News and Sky News you get much more 'Standard English' spoken (perhaps the same on radio), as if the squadrons of regional accent reporters are just wheeled out for daytime use – when the majority of the population would be awake.

When listening to the news or weather, you'll get *ăffta-noon*, *băth*, and a dreadful *for-căssed*, said almost aggressively or angrily, with the emphasis on the 'kăssed', hurled at the listener like a short, sharp venomous attack. Talking about Scottish presenters and the weather, Carol Kirkwood may be chirpy and charming but I find her extremely irritating in the 'weather is more "low-cal" (local) than you think' shots, where one neighbour is in the sunshine and the one in the next door garden is standing in pouring rain. As if English people have nothing better to do except muse about the weather (which often they don't!). Carol invites those watching in a thick Scottish brogue to 'Become a BBC Weather Watcher' and 'Join in the Nation's favourite conversation'! So then you can '*pawst fawtos*' of the nation's weather… Still, the *pownd* (rhymes with hound) in your pocket in England is the same (?) as the pownd (rhymes with owned) in your pocket in Scotland.

Why do weather forecasters (or fore-căss-ters) always talk about 'patchy' rain? Perhaps because if a swathe of rain is expected in some areas but not others, if it is 'patchy', it might explain why it *doesn't* rain in your particular patch. Clouds are always 'working their way' across different regions. Low pressure 'will bring some moody weather', and some 'lumpy clouds'. 'A spot of rain or drizzle here and there, so not wall-to-wall sunshine for today.' 'There'll be a chănce of some showers poppin' up, some driftin' eastwards, all the while.' 'Temperatures will be fallin' away tonight'… then hoverin' around 10 degrees Celsius, 50 degrees fara-night' (Fahrenheit).

I'd only switched on the TV for a couple of minutes when the BBC weatherman pointed at a lurid, Munch-like yellow swirl behind him and said, 'That's the rem-e-nants of Hurricane Matthew.' Unless he'd just been watching *The Revenant*, so subconsciously suggesting the pronunciation 'rem-e-nants' to himself, it's a remnant! In case of doubt Edvard Munch, who'd likely scream too if you said 'munch' as in 'crunch' when it's Edvard with a 'v', surname pronounced 'Munk', not monk either, but rhymes with punk with a northern accent.

## How to speak good English

A good way to learn how to speak good English (apart from being sent to a good school like Eton) is to switch on to BBC *Parliament* and just listen. You will hear a wide range of regional accents, including the well moderated tones of David Cameron (temporarily 'on leave'), a man who would never like Tony Blair affect a working-cläss (sorry, working cläss) accent to please his supporters. The MP Keith Vaz, as well as being an excellent (ex-)chair of the Commons Home Affairs Select Committee, speaks English, that is pronounces it, better than most English people. As a role model as to how English is spoken and pronounced, Keith Vaz (alma mater: Gonville and Caius [pronounced *keys*] College, Cambridge) is right up there with the very best (as is David Cameron). Urbane, courteous and well mannered, there is nothing 'flighty' or off-putting about the way Vaz (pronounced like the last syllable in 'razzmatazz') speaks English whereas Joanna Lumley, say, can sound 'plummy' and patronising. His earlier support of homeopathy was perhaps misguided, and perhaps he could have been a little more forgiving when Salman Rushdie published *The Satanic Verses*. (As of late 2016, Keith Vaz stepped down from the select committee he chaired following damaging allegations in a Sunday newspaper. 'Those who hold others to account,' he notably opined, 'must themselves be accountable.')

Whilst on the subject of (home affairs) select committee members, of whom there are many notable members, anyone who wants to understand the workings of our singularly unique parliamentary system(s) need only tune in to the BBC's *Parliament* channel. It should be mandatory viewing for all sixth formers. Note to Chuka Umunna (pron. uh-moon-ah): please note that it's a 'PLETH-ora' and not a 'ple-THORA' (as in a huge amount of something). Able lawyers don't tend to be too hot in English. In fact, I think Lord Denning is to be congratulated, simply because he began a summing up in one famous case by stating, 'It was bluebell time in Kent...' I forget the name of the case [*Lewis v Averay 1971*] but I never forgot the picture in my mind of Kentish bluebells in a sylvan wood (that must be a tautology).

In case anyone thinks gender comes into the argument, and there are more males than females mentioned, may I just mention a formidable member of the Public Accounts Committee, the astute Labour MP chair, Meg Hillier (alma mater: St Hilda's, Oxford). She questions like a terrier in a hurry, snapping out another question (and one after that) before there's been a complete answer to the previous one. She likes to 'cut through the narrative' and focus on the detail. If you think Margaret Thatcher could be overbearing at times, try watching Meg Hillier in action on the *Parliament* channel.

(Despite his erudite learning, one could never recommend Sir Peregrine Gerard Worsthorne, the well-known nonagenarian British journalist, writer and broadcaster as a role model for English pronunciation, except only for cruelly satirical reasons. Even those great masters of the stage, Laurence Olivier, John Gielgud and Ralph Richardson now sound stilted and dated. Finding modern equivalents is not easy but no doubt there are many fine young actors (and not just actors but 'ordinary people' too, you could easily make the numbers huge), who could be nominated. Think of Ralph Fiennes, Tom Hiddleston, et al. In looking at 'actors' in the House of Commons – even the dulcet tones of a Jacob Rees-Mogg (alma mater: Eton College, Trinity College, Oxford) seem a hark-back to a donnish cloister in the sixties or a monkish monastery in Somerset.)

Jacob Rees-Mogg is a favourite with parliamentary sketch writers; they like to refer to him as 'the honourable member for the early 20th century'. It has been bruited that he wears wing-collared pyjamas in bed - a splendid apocryphal story. Listening to ITV's *News at Ten* recently, I picked up on Rageh Omaar's good diction and panache in speaking. Straightaway I noted a 'glarse-go' rather than glăss-go for Glasgow. With a quick search on Wikipedia (invaluable), I discovered why. Omaar went to two independent schools (the Dragon School in Oxford and Cheltenham College). This excellent education was completed at his alma mater, New College, Oxford.

The son of a wealthy businessman from Somalia, Omaar moved to the UK at the age of two. As a Sunni Muslim, he has strong leanings in both camps, so to speak, Somalia and England. He worked for the BBC for a time but eventually left, suggesting that 'the BBC working environment was somewhat exclusivist on a class basis' and because of his public school education, 'he was guilty of this as well to some degree'. (I thought Greg Dyke [former director general at the BBC] had changed all that...)

I was tempted to suggest that you can be a 'posh' presenter on the BBC or ITV if you are black or coloured. If white, it's possible you could be axed for being too white and posh. For example, Edward Stourton (alma mater: Trinity College, Cambridge) was allegedly dropped from Radio 4's *Today* programme for being too 'posh', though this was denied.

Colour is no bar to the top in politics, however. The redoubtable Tory MP, Kwasi Kwarteng, born in London of Ghanaian parents is a notable example. His educational background is like a roll call of academic success, from Eton College to Trinity College, Cambridge, and then Harvard University, followed by a PhD in Economic History back at Cambridge. There are some 68 ethnic minority Members of the House of Lords and around 65 ethnic minority MPs in the House of Commons.

It's probably unfair and rash to single out any members of parliament as there are so many with illustrious careers, so only a mention of three here: Lord Desai (Meghnad Desai, Baron Desai) tends to ramble on a bit in parliamentary debates; Lord Ahmad (Tariq Ahmad, Baron Ahmad of Wimbledon) could brush up a little on his grammar; in a debate about vulnerable children, I heard him say that something must be done to help 'them children'; and I would never have guessed that Lord Coe (Sebastian Newbold Coe, Baron Coe) can claim ethnic minority status through his mother, who was of half Indian descent born to a Punjabi father.

Most MPs have their favourite seat or place in the House of Commons. Jacob Rees-Mogg likes a position 'up on a corner' (a rather inadequate description). By contrast, Dennis Skinner, Labour MP for Bolsover (hence 'The Beast of Bolsover') has not only a favourite perch but a favourite 'posture', which is usually leaning forward eagerly and attentively, quite good as he must be about 85.

One of the clearest speakers in the House of Commons is actually the Speaker himself, John Bercow. Just to be clear, that's Ber-co and not Ber-cow. When not yelling mellifluously at barracking members, he has a nice line in astute observations, usually delivered with stylish good humour. In November 2016, I happened to listen to him in full swing at Prime Minister's Questions (PMQ). He was berating an MP for gettimg too excited (I don't recall his name.) ORDER! ORDER! ORDER! [MP's name]. You are in a very emotional state. I normally regard you as a cerēbral denizen of the House. Regain your composure man!'

## Tony Blair goes to school

Tony Blair was sent as a boarder to a top boarding school in Scotland, Fettes (pron. FETT-is) College. The school has an illustrious history and notable alumni. It is worth searching Google for an image – you will see it is a vast, extraordinary building, a Scottish baronial castle, in parts in the style of a French chateau, almost preposterous in its expansive grandeur.

*Tatler Magazine* once described it (in 2007) as a place that 'used to have a hearty, rugger-bugger, Caledonian image'. A true English gentleman should be comfortable with the way his voice sounds, and can keep the company of lairds or labourers and be an equal among them. He should not make crass attempts to feign a working-class accent, to make his listeners more 'comfortable' in their own skins. As Kipling said, 'If you can talk with crowds and keep your virtue, Or walk with kings – nor lose the common touch…' By the way, if you say 'crass' to rhyme with 'arse' you are definitely an old-style Tory who needs outing, the sooner the better. It's crăss, you ass! (Similarly, the 'old school', say those of similar age when Lord Carrington was Defence Secretary in the early 1970s, liked to refer to 'Yer-rup' instead of 'Your-rup' (Europe) long before Breggsit, I mean Brexit, was even contemplated.)

Ed Milliband did much the same just before the 2015 General Election when cosying up to Russell Brand and constructing hideous mockney sentences in the latter's bedroom. Long before the 'Bacon Sandwich' incident, Edward Milliband was climbing the ranks, so to speak, via Corpus Christi College, Oxford and the London School of Economics. (By the way, is it *vee-a*, or *vye-a* (via)? Probably both are correct but I prefer vye-a.) The *Oxford Dictionary* prefers 'vy-a' if that's any clearer.

Tony Blair's best friend in their Scottish schooldays was Charlie Falconer, Baron Falconer of Thoroton, PC, QC. The two men also share the annoying habit (to southern ears at least) of pronouncing words like 'sure' as SHU-AH – or add an sh to sewer so it sounds like 'shewer' or 'shoe-a'. Gordon Brown, being Scottish, has the same trait, as does Tim Farron, the Liberal Democrat leader with another word. ('If you want Britain to be safe and *se-cu-ah*, stay in the EU.') It sounds so laboured; it's almost as if the men enjoy saying it: '*We want this government to be SHU-AH to protect the interests of the ordinary working person...*'

Of course if they want to say SHU-AH for 'sure', it's their right but I find it comes across as slightly pompous but they do love it: '*We must be SHU-AH...*'

## Some American pronunciations

In the United States, there are some unfamiliar pronunciations of English words but no one objects. Words like 'fragil' (sounds like frah-jill) for fragile (fra-jyle), 'u-man/ youman' for human, 've-hic-al' for vehicle. They are very fond of talking about DICK-tators, with the stress on 'dick', whereas really we like the stress after dick as in dic/ TATor. They like 'urbs like oREG-ano rather than herbs like or-e-GAN-o. There are hundreds more like that.

If you have been brought up in Britain watching a lot of American TV shows, you may have picked up a mistaken way to say 'congratulations', without you even having noticed it. I don't know why but many Americans appear to throw in a 'd', so they seem to say, '*congradulations*'. Americans talk of Putin being in *Moss-cow* and how a car has a *ch-assis*, like the 'ch' in chip, rather than a chassis (*shass-ee*).

(With reference to the Russian president, a senior diplomat branded Vladimir Putin a 'liar' and a 'thug', after the seizure of the Crimean Peninsula (2014). Just who was this man? Sir Peter Westmacott, GCMG, the UK ambassador to the US (alma mater: New College, Oxford), who was awarded the Knight Grand Cross of the Order of St Michael and St George (GCMG) in 2016. The British can be outspoken. To be told by 'a GCMG man' that you are a liar and a thug is surely the most damning, *persona non grata* remark one could ever make to anyone.)

Quite why a 'z' is a 'zee' to them I just don't know. And a văse, now that's a vāse (rhymes with haze). If an American is going to a roller derby in Berkeley Square he's not going to a derby (rhymes with far) in Berkeley (pronounced as Barclee) Square but to a derby (to rhyme with Herbie) in Berkeley (to rhyme with berk) Square.

## English pronunciations awry!

I suppose my 'gripe' is not with 'foreigners' mispronouncing English words (we all do that when abroad) but British people pronouncing quite ordinary words wrongly, when they should know better.

Take for example the word 'RHEToric' – the stress is more or less equal – but with more stress on the first syllable. But we also have the adjective rhetorical, where the stress is rhet/ORICAL, with the 't' carrying over to stress the 'oric' in rhe-torical.

A new pronunciation has crept in. I heard it in June 2015, when Vernon Coaker, a worthy Labour MP, got up in the House of Commons to talk about how he'd had to listen to so much 'rhet-*ORIC*', and how he was getting fed up with it. Is it such a difficult or abstruse word? I don't think so but Vernon Coaker has his own ideas.

The BBC *South at Six* newsreader, Fred Dinenage, who has the idiosyncratic habit of stretching out his left arm over the notes he is reading on the desk before him, arching the left hand down on the table rather grandiosely, a habit also favoured by Gordon Brown, recently described a creature (I know it as a *tort-us* [tortoise]) – as a –'tor-toyse'. Does it matter? Only that it's a bit uncool – or 'naff' in Fred's terms – 'unstylish, lacking taste, inferior'. I had thought incidentally that turquoise, the magnificently exotic greeny-blue mineral, was pronounced *tur-quaaz* after the French but modern usage in Britain seems to favour *tur-kwoys*, sadly.

Wishing to offend as few people as possible, I think I will have to stay away from regional accents, that is complaining about them, as I have no objections to Dorset yokels *à la* William Barnes, and one must surely be proud in some ways of the broad Yorkshire accent, loved by so many. The Liverpudlian (Scousers) accent has always sounded to me as whiningly annoying (but see below) and the Brummie accent as plain ridiculous. In truth, there are so many regional accents, let alone dialects, that it's most unfair to criticise any of them unduly – I mean one just gets used to hearing, 'He's just tekking the mickey' or 'Thar'll do nicely, laddie' that – it's best not to go there.

## From Liverpool and proud of it

(Scousers roll their 'r's, like the Scots; just ask a Scouser to say 'great' – it rolls nicely off the tongue. Liverpudlians are proud of their heritage. I asked one young woman with jet black hair, lively shining eyes, and black eyebrows that looked painted on with a 6mm brush, 'Are you proud of your accent?' She gave it a little thought, then said, 'No, but I'm proud of where I cŭme from.' I said, 'Why are you so proud of Liverpool?' She answered, 'I'm proud of my city. We fight. We all fight for whaar we believe in. We don't take nuthink lying down.' I say 'roll on the northern powerhouse' – to utilise some of that raw, positive and powerful energy.)

Instead, I think I will just have to list a number of 'gripes', a gripe meaning to complain about something in a persistent, irritating way. That doesn't sound very hopeful either so I shall have to add a sprinkling of humour here and there to make the whole more palatable.

## How to start a controversy

One way is to pit those who say con*trov*-ersy against those who say con-tro-ver-sy (equal stress all 4 syllables) (the former is still questionably preferable, that's *pref*erable and not pre*fer*able).

Another is to suggest that the longest word most often used by the working classes is either *relegate* or *relegation*. The word 'relegation' is very popular among the football classes; in some families it might even be learnt by three- or four-year-olds. It is also uttered as a kind of talismanic curse of something simply dreadful that might happen to their favourite team in the future, as in, '*Oh no, we're gonna be relega'ed!*'

Another is to write a book subtitled *The Pocket Book of (Proper) English Pronunciation*. It's a sure way to court excessive trolling or brickbats in the street…

Does this sound a little miss-CHEEV-**I**-us or MISS-chiv-us to you? Or even *mischeevyious*? Where did the extra 'ee' sound come from in 'mischievous'? Try to say *miss-chiff* (mischief) and not *Miss Cheef.* Another word where an extra syllable creeps in is 'communial', as in 'We have a communial garden here.' It's comm-UN-al (communal). Perhaps it's wrong to pick on Londoners from Romford, Essex but a fair few of them in my opinion would think you were speaking the Queen's English if you asked for 'directions to a pub with a communial garden'. Eponymous Romford Man also likes to talk about the 'thee-atta' (thee-ATT-ter) rather than 'thee-ah-ter'. On good authority, there are actually many people from the Romford area who say 'thee-eh-ter'!

I like to start *projects* – but not in the Scottish style of TV presenter and journalist Kirsty Wark, who prefers to talk about 'Prō-ject Fear'. Perhaps they have more prō-jects in Scotland and fewer prŏ-jects in England. Like many a Scot, Kirsty Walk pronounces 'crude' oil (rhymes with rude) as crŭd (rhymes with hood).

On the subject of prōjects, Hairy Biker (Dave Myers) in a new guise as 'The Hairy Builder' made a programme on the restoration of Castle Drogo on Dartmoor, a grandiose granite country house and castle (the last castle built in England), designed by Edwin Lutyens (lutchens or luhchens). For him, it was a very *'excitin' prōject'*; it was for me too, because his enthusiasm and good humour are catching. He went onto the flat roof of the castle to see new 'ash-felt' laid down. I don't confess to be a building expert but as far as I know 'asphalt' has neither ash nor felt in it.

Some of the building materials he discussed were measured in kilograms (sounded like kee-lo-grams). I'm sure it's, say, £15 a kee-lo (kilo), not a kĭl-lo) but 15 kĭlograms rather than 'kee-lo-grams'. For amusement, please listen to this Japanese man pronouncing 'kilogram' for a Japanese audience.[4] It's subtly different. Kilograms, kilometres, kilometers and speedometers would need an entire chapter so, *to be honest*, I think that's enough for the time being.

This project is an attempt to sift through the media of news presenting and radio programmes and pick out a few cherries (or are they poison berries?) worth a quick comment. Carping and critics go hand in hand. Most people have few sympathies for cavilling critics, whether lay or professional. In fact, none of this is intended in any way to criticise. I think Shakespeare has taught us that the English language can be bent, twisted and cajoled into all sorts of shapes and new forms and still be beautiful.

Try to imagine a Dali-like ear floating mid-air next to a radio or TV set. Some sounds are mellifluous, some average, but many are just wrong! On respected Radio 4, a presenter talking on a health programme discusses the effects of '*in-shoo-lin*' (insulin); another talks about a '*melly*' (to rhyme with jelly) (which might have happened in Ronnie Scott's Jazz Club if George Melly had been playing), when *mell-ay* (mêlée) was meant; and once a Sky News presenter mentioned that someone had been chosen as the new royal '*pătt-ron*' (instead of pā-tron). She did change it to 'pātron' but only when another newsreader corrected her. (A 'stickler' might say, perhaps she had been holidaying in France, guided to a pleasant restaurant by Rick Stein where she met 'le patron' and got the two mixed up.)

## A note on the complicated nature of linguistics

Linguistics is probably a more academic subject than many others. Just a quick example as to why *The Mischievious Athalete: The Pocket Book of (Proper) English Pronunciation* does not include material that linguists would love. I've decided to abbreviate the title. Let's say, we haven't forgotten *The Mischievious Athalete*; he or she will appear from time to time, but I think it's simpler in the text to refer to *The Pocket Book of (Proper) English Pronunciation*.

Take for example, the '*wh*' pronunciation, which in Scotland and Ireland is unlike the English '*wh*' sound – which is why Scots talk about '*hwhales*' but for the English a 'whale' is pronounced as '*wail*'. There's even a name for '*wh*' – it's a diagraph. Here are some linguists' terms associated with the diagraph '*wh*':

*the wine-whine merger*
*voiceless stops*
*a labialized velar fricative*
*glide cluster reduction*
*Proto-Indo-European consonant*
*Grimm's Law*
*phonological merger*
*voiced labio-velar approximant*

Hence the decision 'not to go there'. It would take too long to understand and years to get right and, more importantly, any book would only be read passionately by linguists. If you are not convinced, 'voiceless plosives', 'creaky voice', 'vellarised allophones' and 'dipthongised vowels' are all terms in the phonologist's toolkit (phonology being the study of the structure of speech sounds, and the way in which they are combined). Let's move on, shall we?

## A note on pronunciation guides on the net

Not too long ago, I met 'EmmaSaying' as in www.emma saying.com, an online dictionary of pronunciation project.

Over 180,000 video pronunciation videos have been uploaded since late 2012 with over 121m video views, averaging nearly 6m views a month. Generally English pronunciation is given with some American alternatives. It's accurate although I did find one mistake. Coutts is pronounced like 'Coats' in the video. Perhaps right for a surname but not for Coutts Bank, a very old and private bank, founded in 1692. I'm sure the right way to pronounce Coutts is Kuts (rhymes with nuts). Someone asked the same question on Mumsnet and there was just one reply: '*the same as boots*', which it certainly isn't. Coots are water birds found on lakes and rivers. But, on the other hand, and not satisfied with my suggestion it should be 'Cutts', I rang the Strand branch. The receptionist had a distinct Estuary English accent. She answered, 'Nah, it's Coots.' I said, 'Has it always been coots?' 'Yeah.' 'Do all the top managers and staff say coots?' I asked cheekily, about to be hoist with my own petard. 'Yeah, for as long as I can reemember [*sic*].' 'Oh well, I suppose I can't argue with that. Thanks anyway.'

EmmaSaying is a very useful tool when you can't quite remember how to pronounce a word or have forgotten altogether.

There is some satirical subterfuge too on the net. Try searching for this: 'Pronunciation Manual Astronaut'.[5] It's so silly it's actually quite funny. Funnier still is this effort at pronouncing 'penis'.[6] Also try 'Benedict Cumberbatch', 'cappuccino', 'zucchini', etc. Many people must have looked up these 'Pronunciation Manual' words from around the world, thinking they were about to hear the real thing. That's a lot of head scratching.

## A note on phonetics and vowels

The International Phonetic Alphabet (commonly known as IPA), which can be used for the phonetic transcription of a language, is not used here. The system can be used for the phonetic transcription of *any* language (surely a feat in itself), has been in use since 1888, and is mainly based on the Latin alphabet. It reflects only the parts of speech that 'are part of oral language'.[7]

The IPA is not just used by linguists but by actors, teachers, students, singers, translators and 'masochistic lucubrators' – the lexicographers who spend hours, even years, compiling dictionaries.

Just a brief glance at the subject on Wikipedia[8] reveals it's quite complicated. Besides the oral speech we use, in order 'to represent additional qualities of speech, such as tooth gnashing [*sic*], lisping, and sounds made with a cleft lip and cleft palate, an extended set of symbols, the extensions to the International Phonetic Alphabet, may be used'.[9]

Instead of any attempt at IPA symbols, *The Pocket Book of (Proper) English Pronunciation* uses a very simple system, which is very much left to the reader's intelligence! Some parts of words are capitalised to show the stress in particular words. For example, note the word 'rebel' (noun) but 'to re-BEL' (verb), but this is by no means consistently applied.

Vowels may be short or long, and shown thus: căt *but* cāper, măt *but* māte, băth *or* bāth (north/south). To help show the right pronunciation, sometimes 'sounds like' tactics are employed.

If you would really like some pronunciation practice, try the poem in Appendix I. It's said that if you can pronounce every word correctly, your English is better than 90 per cent of the UK's (native) population (*see* Appendix 1). I think the figure may be a little more. Don't you? (I mean the true percentage is likely to be higher than 90 per cent.)

You can listen to one version here. It's quite clear, if with a slight American accent: https://youtube.com/#/watch?v=49XAyJLCD3E.

You can try the pronunciation yourself at the end of the book in Appendix 1. The author of this unique poem was Dutchman Gerard Nolst Trenité. It's already not far off being 100 years old, having been written and published in 1922 in a book with the graphic title of *The Chaos* (of English Pronunciation!). It points out irregularities and pitfalls of spelling and pronunciation, written from the point of view of a non-native speaker or someone learning English. The poem was originally published as an appendix in a book of pronunciation exercises, then reprinted in another book, *Drop Your Foreign Accent.*[10]

# CHAPTER ONE

*Ladies in Waitrose buying scōnes – 'Ma'am' rhymes with jam – a 'weasel' with words – cold grouse and a good claret for breakfast – 'Must get in me [sic] car' – Chilcot report – acting school*

You're shopping in Waitrose and find yourself next to two well dressed ladies at the cream tea and cake counter. One sees a scone, with a dollop of cream on one side and a smudge of jam on the other. 'Oh,' says one to her friend, 'I do love SCŌNES with a little cream and strawberry jam.'

Now I am standing next to her. Should I tell her it's not SCŌNES but SCŎNES? The former belongs to those who like to effect 'airs and graces', like Mrs Hyacinth Bucket (pron. 'Bouquet') from the sitcom *Keeping Up Appearances*) or the plain ignorant. A scŏne is a scŏne, bless it, and not a scōne. (I did tell her and she thanked me!) Waitrose was founded by Wallace Waite and Arthur Rose, with David Taylor opening their first shop in Acton, West London. Although you could argue the name is Wait(e)

Rose, it's *definitely* to be pronounced Way-trose and not Weigh'(glottal stop) Rose, this pronunciation verging on the unfortunate chav(ish).

## 'Ma'am' rhymes with jam

A similar attempt to sound correct (mistaken) is made by those people who dream of meeting the Queen, and addressing her as 'Ma'am' to rhyme with farm. A Buckingham Palace protocol note in the early 1990s directed that Her Majesty be addressed as 'Ma'am' (to rhyme with jam). I don't know why but suddenly I found myself singing a tune just like Paul Simon's *50 Ways to Leave Your Lover*: 'Get out the jam, Ma'am, Just slip out the back, Jack ... Don't need to be coy, Roy ... Just get out the jam, Ma'am.'

A similar mistake happens with the word 'gala', a festive occasion or celebration. Miners used to have them and still do (e.g. the Durham Miners' Gala). In America, it's called a 'gay-la' but the right British pronunciation has got to be 'gahla'.

My dear father came from a generation that liked to say 'Majorca' with a hard 'j' (as in *jaw*) and anyone who said otherwise was dismissed as effete. It's anyway now better known as Mallorca, with the double 'l' pronounced like 'y'. Similar arguments happened with 'margarine', although I seem to remember it began life when I was a teenager with a soft 'g' (imported from America), which later became hard, so in effect the other way round. Another classic example of the 'old school' being out of touch was when, in a debate at the Oxford Union, Ted Heath, the former conservative PM, mentioned various countries he had been involved with, including one SRY-Lanka (rather than SREE/Lanka). However, it's fair to say that the country previously known as Ceylon changed its name to Sri Lanka only in 1972 when it became a republic, just three years before Heath's speech – so perhaps in 1972 people were probably not that clear whether the pronunciation was sry (to rhyme with eye) or sree.

## A 'weasel' with words

One of the greatest 'weasels' with words has got to be Tony Blair (alma mater: St John's College, Oxford, Inns of Court). His attempts at 'speaking in the vernacular', presumably to sound *au fait* with the working classes, despite having gone to Fettes, verged on the pathetic. You'd never catch Sir Nicholas Soames saying, 'We have an army capable of fighting the infidel from Păkistăn to Afghănistăn.' Poor Tony always seemed to struggle to 'en-shuah' that 'stan', as in the man's name (Stanley) was always his usage, even though you can hear many Pakistanis who say they come from Păkistăn or Afghanis who say they are from Afghānistān. One short and one long in both cases is perhaps the preferred usage. Priti Patel MP has got it right, I think. She talks of 'Afghăns' but 'Afghănistăn' – although most Afghans themselves are likely to say 'Afghăns' in their own language. How correct my opinion is re Priti Patel is subject to some 'dubitation' (a word I learnt from Boris Johnson). Her religion is Hinduism, and she is of Indian origin via Uganda to Britain. There are indeed many Pakistanis who use two long 'a's' (Pākistān), although how much the educated classes try to ape their former colonial masters, or at least did at one time, is open to question. Note how the term of abuse 'Paki' is always short. No one ever talks of a 'Pāki' (perhaps admittedly because Paki with a long 'a' sounds like 'parky' [chilly] or 'parkie' [a park-keeper]).

## The best breakfast?
## Cold grouse and a good claret

Incidentally, one of the cleverest things ever said by Sir Nicholas was his preferred breakfast fare: 'Cold grouse and a good claret'.

Politicians certainly are nowadays a very varied lot. On the night David Cameron left government and Theresa May became Prime Minister, I switched on my TV to hear a Labour MP complaining about intimidation in the party. She described this as 'dis-guustin' bee'aveyur' and opined that the 'poliical' climate was unhealthy. 'People knows [sic] this should stop,' she said earnestly. Really, some of this must be down to the 'qual-i-ee' of the incumbents. (I think the MP's name was Angela Rayner.)

*But*, I run ahead of myself. This wonderful word is an old favourite, mainly of Labour supporters. They tend in the main to use certain stock phrases, as if it might help their thought processes. One of these (leaving aside *but* for the moment) is 'about'.

You'll hear things like, 'It's not *about* (or abou') helping the working clǎss, it's *about* stoppin' the Tories from 'avin' a stranglehold over ower guvernment.' 'It's abou' taking the fight to the Tories.' Forms of spoken argument nearly always seem to discuss what things are about or not about. 'It's not abou' personali'ies, it's abou' policies.' Now and again, you will get a chummy, '*Look*, it's not abou'…' There is also the more mildly authoritative to a TV reporter, '*Listen*…' (Angela Eagle) or '*Look*…' (David Milliband). There is also the pointless rhetorical question, '*D'you know what?* followed by a statement of party faith, dogma, or just simple observation. *'Not on our watch!'* The British love their seagoing history.

## 'Must get in me [*sic*] car'

When Angela Eagle was questioned during her leadership bid (it's also true for some other Labour MPs) – she happened to be hurrying somewhere – she excused herself, saying she must 'get in me [*sic*] car', as she had to be 'gettin' on with fightin' the Tories', as if 'fighting the Tories' was the one great mission in her life.

To return to 'but'. The 'but' I find myself objecting to has two syllables, and is made to sound like a very long word. It is used to put or make a counter-argument in one sentence, a kind of inferior reasoning method. So, 'My work in the department has been fun *buu-uuut* it is now time to move on.' The first syllable is usually higher in tone than the second. Lancashire-born Andy Burnham MP (alma mater: Fitzwilliam College, Cambridge) uses it quite a lot in the House of Commons.

Regarding lost consonants, the London mayor Sadiq Khan loves gettin' things done – whether it's movin', speakin' to the public, or just talkin', he's your man (Priti Patel similarly). There's one particularly annoying female Sky TV news presenter who also speaks in the same way. When covering the new ministerial appointments in Downing Street, after Theresa May took office, she dropped her phone, saying, 'Shi', just dropped me phone'; the main Sky anchorman had to cover for her, suggesting the bad language might have been a comment from a passerby. (The presenter was Beth Rigby, a senior political correspondent no less, who sounds dourly earnest much of the time, as if overly concerned like a glum Cassandra, and is great on such lines as, 'They're worried about the fundin', really worried.') *Note:* 'respeck', that is Estuary English for respect, for Beth (alma mater: Cambridge University, University of London).

## The Chilcot report - a study for acting school?

So, *'All the world's a stage and all the men and women are merely players…'* The world *is* a stage, and we *are* all actors in it. Whilst on the subject of acting, if I were running a drama school (I am not a very good actor, so it's preposterously unlikely), I would steer all would be actors to watch Tony Blair's speech on the Iraq Inquiry – his response to the Chilcot report. It is surely a master class that all serious students of acting should see. The fluttering eyelids, the high drama, a voice cracking with emotion, it's on YouTube[1] but rather long at 1 hour 49 minutes.

# CHAPTER TWO

*Care needed when addressing people – black spider memos – how to write a letter to a member of the Royal Family – Taff, Jock and Ginger –* Debrett's Peerage *– two important words to remember – confusion with accents – more presenters with regional accents – clichés and stock phrases – goodbye to i.e., e.g. and etc. – pronunciation of some letters and vowels – haitch – hypercorrection – eye-ther or ee-ther, US pronunciations – some English 'howlers' – a few bêtes noires – counterintuitive pronunciations*

Y OU NEED TO TAKE care when addressing people. They deserve the respect of getting their names right, although thank goodness many of the laborious and tedious (even servile) forms of address that were common in the previous age of deference have disappeared. Sometimes, they survive, as witness Andy Burnham's letter of reply (see below) written to Prince Charles, revealed in what became known as the 'black spider memos' – a reference to Prince Charles's spidery black handwriting in a series of letters fired off to government ministers and others. Prince Charles was (and probably still is) in the habit of writing at least one thousand letters a year, complaining about, or commenting on, public matters. Some hacks took to describing the Prince as the 'Prince of Wails'.

If you happened to be sitting in the House of Lords, and wanted to address the Archbishop of Canterbury in a debate, is there a 'correct' form of address? Yes, bound to be and it's 'The Most Reverend Primate, the Archbishop of Canterbury'. Sometimes this is shortened to 'Your Grace' or even 'Archbishop'. He has the legal right to sign his name as '*Cantuar*', which is Latin for Canterbury. Retired bishops are referred to as 'The Right Reverend'.

Andy Burnham (who is actually a very good MP) ended his letter: 'I have the honour to remain, Sir, Your Royal Highness's most humble and obedient servant.' Tony Blair was less formal, ending his letters to the Prince with 'Yours ever, Tony'.

## Black spider memos/Royal letter writing

It took ten years and a Freedom of Information Act request from *Guardian* journalists and over £274,000 in legal costs for the public to see just 27 of the black spider memos, along with some redactions. The case was fought by the government (on quasi-behalf of Prince Charles) all the way from a freedom of information tribunal to the High Court, the Appeal Court, and then finally to the highest court in the land, the Supreme Court.

Incidentally, in terms of how to address strangers (and royalty), there is an apt Clarence House website, for younger people, on 'How to write a letter to a member of the Royal Family!'[1] There are nine instructions, including, 'If you are writing to a member of the Royal Family, you can start your letter with "Your Royal Highness", or "Sir" or "Ma'am" (*jam*).' You must 'write clearly'. You should 'use paragraphs' and 'Don't forget your stamp!' The address to be put on the envelope is suitably grand too: Clarence House, London SW1A 1BA.

The British use many familiar words when addressing strangers, say, in pubs. Sometimes the words used can be offensive; many times those using them probably don't even notice they might cause offence.

Common words used are: pal, mate, pet, fella, friend, chŭck, buddy, 'no worries, bud', etc. The appellation 'mate' is very common, and is not usually offensive – quite the opposite. Of course it depends on the context. To call someone 'pal' can raise the hackles, as in, 'Now look here, pal…' (it can sound menacing).

Unless auditioning for a TV reality show, it is highly advisable to avoid using these words, for example in a television interview, or you will sound decidedly 'common'. Equally, never be servile and address anyone as 'Sir', unless of tender years. 'Sir' is acceptable in a service connotation, say if you are a hotel manager or shop attendant. The Americans seem to love addressing anyone as 'Sir' much of the time. Sir Philip Green addressed some members of the select committee questioning him over the BHS affair as 'Sir', unusual for someone called as a witness (except in courts of law), but I suspect it was not without a tinge of mockery.

(On the other hand, calling a suspect 'Sir' is magnificent when it's Peter Falk as Lieutenant (pronounced lootenant in the US) Colombo doing the questioning.)

## Taff, Jock and Ginger

The communications regulator Ofcom has issued some new guidelines in *Attitudes to potentially offensive language and gestures on TV and radio*.[2] To call someone from Wales 'Taff' is seen as more offensive than 'Jock', and 'Jock' is not wrong, it just depends on the context. 'Ginger' was described as 'a comical term', nothing more than a 'humorous insult'.

Scottish people, or 'Jocks', seem congenitally attached to the word 'wee', for little. It's 'wee this' and 'wee that'; it's enough to drive one barmy (a word popular with Brummies) but I don't think today there would be many 'takers' for essayist Charles Lamb's (1775–1834) view: 'I have been trying all my life to like Scotchmen, and am obliged to desist from the experiment in despair.' (Of course, Charles Lamb didn't know Andy Murray.)

You can say 'nigga' if you are a rapper 'singing' a song. But definitely not 'nigger'; of course, no rapper is going to say 'nigger', as speakers of London or Estuary English would pronounce it as 'nigga' anyway.

## Forms of address and *Debrett's Peerage*

Forms of address in the upper classes are ridiculously long winded in many cases, and as this is only a pocketbook, I think I can safely avoid them. You can always check on the internet if you need to find out how to address 'your liege lord'.

You *might* also care to look into *Debrett's Peerage & Baronetage* – but only if you are incredibly desperate. Its website has 31,000 pages of advice (including etiquette) and profiles. You might also try consulting 'style guru' Peter York, best known for co-authoring *The Official Sloane Ranger Handbook*. As it was first published in 1982, it's probably out of date.

A later book by Peter York, published in 2007 had the title, *Cooler, Faster, More Expensive: Return of the Sloane Ranger* [where are they now?]. The back cover gave a list of its essential reading, such as:

- The Latest Guide to What Really Matters
- Where to holiday (Mustique, Val d'Isère or Rock)
- What to eat (organic veg or rare breeds)
- What to wear (Chlöe and Dubarry)
- Who to idolise (Prince Charles, Zac Goldsmith or Beyoncé)
- Where to do rehab
- The problem with Kate

All of which shows how quickly things become out-moded, out of date, and dare I say it, déclassé (see p. 77). *Peter York's Hipster Handbook* (2016) on BBC Four, how-ever, was authentically insightful, and bang on-trend.

*Note:* I can thank my daughter for 'putting me straight' on a number of things. When I was extolling the virtues of my old school, she said, 'Get over it, Dad.' When I was recounting the number of new projects I had in the pipeline, she merely told me, 'Dad, get a life.' This was just after studying playwright Arthur Miller's *Death of a Salesman* for her A levels. '*Willy Loman!*' she exclaimed. 'Dad, you're *exactly* like him!'

## Two Important Words to Remember

These get a quick mention because they are in common usage but slightly 'give the game away' in terms of your background if you use them.

It's quite common to hear some MPs in Parliament (usually Labour MPs) discussing what another member has said, often in this way. 'The honourable member **SAYS** he would try to find an answer; now he SAYS he hasn't got the time.' The fact of the matter is that most educated people will pronounce SAYS as SEZ, to rhyme with fez. So it's, 'He *sez* he would try to find an answer…' If you say, 'He says' it sounds like nursery school English.

The second word to mention here is 'none'. Of course, being a southerner, I am bound to be biased in favour of southern accents, so I apologise. It's just that the Northern way of saying 'none' sounds (to me) clumsy and inelegant. A northerner pronouncing the word '**NONE**' manages to make a mouthful of it, as if the word is half-swallowed in the act of speaking it (much the same applies to the word 'one'). A man who can't avoid sounding a little bit like a northerner, despite his portly and patrician mien is Patrick

Thomas Cormack, The Lord Cormack, and former Tory MP now active in the House of Lords. Why is this, you might ask? Born in Grimsby, and educated at the University of Hull is one good reason. (Another person from Hull (aka Hŭll), and proud of it, is Apprentice star Michelle Dewberry, who is fast making a name for herself again on the Sky TV chat show, *The Pledge*.)

So how should it sound? Think of nuns – but not *nŭns*! Pronouncing the word 'none' as 'nun' sounds so much better than the half-swallowed Northern 'Non', so if you can, stick with, 'Nŭn of my friends has the answer.'

## Confusion with accents

One of the strangest examples of confusion with accents was during a *Newsnight* programme with reporters Evan Davis and Mishal Husain. (For anyone remotely interested in alma maters, a fine selection here: Evan 'clocking up' St John's College, Oxford and Harvard; Mishal Cambridge University, then a master's degree in comparative and international law from the European University Institute, Florence.) There was a discussion about the Navy. Evan said he'd heard that 'some aircrăft had returned to the aircrāft carrier'. In other words, a short 'a' for the first use of 'aircraft' and a long 'a' for the second. I've long had the opinion that the BBC actively encourages short 'a's over long ones. They certainly seem to like words like 'shăft' (rhymes with chiff-*chaff*) instead of 'shāft' with a 'long' 'a'. BBC news presenter Kay Burley makes mistakes from time to time but glosses over them with a kind of faux naivety and couldn't-care-less attitude (on a par with Martine Croxall). She'll happily say, 'Frănce' with a short 'a'. What is it about 'Frănce'? Listen to a Frenchman talk lovingly about 'La Frānce'. I've never heard one yet say 'Frănce' or 'J'habite a *Frănce.*' Martine Croxall is not always the clearest when reading the news. Recently I heard her say (what sounded like) *Brack* Obama ('brack' being a cake or bun with dried fruit). If you think that's amusing, a Tory MP when talking about her leader made the name of the PM sound like 'chorizo May'.

A quick note of approval for *Newsnight*'s James O'Brien – he correctly calls a case 'prŏven' (prohven) and not 'prooven'.

Sky News is just as bad as the BBC for using a plethora of presenters with regional accents. It seems they just love anyone who likes to pronounce 'plants' (rhymes with Nantes in France) as 'plants' (to rhyme with 'ants'). One female news presenter to recommend for clarity, objectivity and a pleasant style of delivery would be Sky's Kimberley Leonard (alma mater: University of Westminster), with Anna Botting (alma mater: St Edmund Hall, Oxford; Cardiff University) not too far behind. Included here should be Emily Maitlis (Queens' College, Cambridge), Sophie Raworth (University of Manchester, City University), and Fiona Bruce (Hertford College, Oxford). The BBC's newsreader Jane Hill is very competent too. BBC's Radio 4 Jane Steele is to be commended for clear pronunciation, as is *Newsnight*'s political editor (and rising star) Nick Watt. The alma maters here were added just before proof stage – out of genuine curiosity. The preponderance of Oxbridge graduates in the top echelons in not an illusion; it's good that a larger intake of state school pupils is actively encouraged.

## Clichés and stock phrases

Apart from dubious pronunciations, try to avoid clichés and 'stock phrases'. 'Definitely' went through a phase not so long ago. It was one of the few words of affirmation capable of being expressed by hoi polloi. 'Are you going to vote for Jeremy Corbyn?' 'Definitely. Yeah. Definitely.' As a most wonderful example of a word 'gone wrong' (a malapropism of sorts) is the man who, when I asked him if he was going to see something or other replied, 'Yes, deferably. Deferably!' Another overused word is obviously. As in, 'Obviously, I am obviously devastated, obviously.'

People confronted with a tiny smidgen of luck will say how they 'just can't *believe* it'. Perhaps Victor Meldrew is to blame. 'Life is a postcode lottery. It's awesome!'

One ever popular hackneyed current phrase is, 'To be honest…' It seems as if a rash of honesty has broken out among all classes. If someone is interviewed for radio or TV on the street, and is asked for an opinion, the answer often begins (and ends with) 'To be honest…'

'What do you think will happen to the UK after Brexit?' 'To be honest, I haven't thought about it much yet – to be honest.'

## Dummer and dummer

Dumbing down is still going on. You can hear the results of slack pronunciation policies and incomplete education any day on the TV or radio. Only last week, a BBC presenter talked of a 'coop' (strictly, a hen house), when she was talking about a military *coup d'état*. It was originally a French word, and the 'p' is silent.

Of course the thicker you are or appear to be on some TV programmes the more popular the show and presenter. Gratuitous swearing is fine and usually gets a 'laff' from the studio audience.

I really don't know where they (the TV producers) find all those lame people to attend shows like *Deal or No Deal*, *Countdown* or *Top Gear*, or even the weird *8 out of 10 Cats Does Countdown* on Channel 4, where you have to put up with host Jimmy Carr laughing like a manically demented hyena. Some must apply months in advance. Do they pay people to attend? (What about those ubiquitous 'whoopers', who always seem to get a whoop in at the end of a programme?) Who would stand behind a motley *Top Gear* crew for however long a programme is and suffer in silence like showroom dummies, whilst (in the old days) Clarkson and Evans et al. mouthed off ad infinitum? How *does* the BBC find over *5,000 people* on a Sunday afternoon to fill the Albert Hall for a *Songs of Praise* episode? Without even a (get your Tommy Cooper hat on) '*Just like that!*'

In July 2016 it was reported[3] that uk.gov web portal sites were to get rid of any Latin abbreviations, such as i.e., e.g. and etc. Why? Because if people living in England had not been brought up speaking English as their first language, they might be 'confused' (favourite word with the British) (hence the success of Confused.com – and let's not even consider 'strutting Dave' in that grotesque Money Supermarket ad), as they would not understand or know the meanings of these weird and random abbreviations etc.

Just for the record, if anyone doesn't know, we have:

- i.e. (abbrev. for *id est*, that is)
- e.g. (abbreviation for *exempli gratia*, for example)
- etc. (abbrev. for *et cetera*, and other things)

## The letter 'e'

An odd one to start with but here are three words which if pronounced in a certain way can reflect what one might describe as a 'plebeian origin'. I doubt you would catch Andrew Mitchell MP (of 'Plebgate' or 'Plodgate' fame) saying words in this way. Do you say you drive a Honda Prēlude or a Prĕlude? The BBC's Chris Rogers thinks it's a pree-lude! That's not just the car. 'The pree-lood to the UN meeting next week gets underway…' It should be 'prell-yude'.

Let's start with the supermarket, Morrisons. You have to listen for this carefully, but in a current TV advert for the supermarket, a toe-curlingly obsequious sounding man, doing the voice over, says, 'MorrEEsons meks (makes) it'. The surname Morrison properly has a short 'i' sound like 'ih'.

A friend of mine sometimes mentions the *Daily Telegraph* but when he says it, it sounds like the *Daily Teleegraph*, which is wrong. Similarly, those who ride around in 'hel*ee*copters'. Frank Field, the commendable Labour MP who sparred mightily with BHS founder Sir Philip Green in a Commons select committee, refers to David Mill-ee-band (Milliband), as do many others. When pronounced 'mill-ee-band', instead of with two short 'i's' (Mĭllĭband), it sounds like an unusual kind of mill-ee-pede (millipede).

Try never to say *bee*-fore (B4), as in 'I've been there bĕfore.' It's a short 'e' (rhymes with biff). As soon as anyone says '*beefore*' aloud in English, it's a sure giveaway of lack of a certain finesse or cachet in speaking but I am also sure that many will disagree. Get a statement like this onto some Channel 4 chat shows, and they'd maul it. '*If I wanna say B4, I'll bluddy well say it, like it's my own business, mate, so shut the f\*\*\* up!*'

'Going to a business ee-vent?' the TV advert asked. One does not go to an ee-vent, but an ĕvent. You can spot a 'local yokel' with most words that begin with *re-* (and *de-*). You may (wrongly) hear ree-member, ree-turn, ree-lease yet we do ask for a ree-fund and a ree-bate. Eton College recently unveiled a new £18 million debating chamber for its pupils. To be sure, if any Eton boy got up and said, 'I am privileged to speak in this dēbating chamber', he would likely be laughed out of the Greek inspired theatre (see also p. 62). Should you have a dispute in the debating theatre, make sure you say 'disPUTE' or 'disPute' but not 'DISS-pewt'!

You can '*ree*cover' (re-cover) a chair but has your health rĕcovered (not 'reecovered') yet? Similarly, one talks of dĕporting someone, who is subject to a *dee*portation (deportation) order. One goes on a dētour but don't let this dĕtract you. Don't say 'ee-leven' either, as in nine, ten, eleven. It's 'e-leven' (sounds like uh-leven). Do you think Trident nuclear submarines are an ēffective dĕterrent or an ĕffective dĕterrent? [If the former, you may be up for *ree-tirement* soon. 'One rĕtires, sir, to a cosy rĕtirement home with a clock for company,' as Jeeves might opine to Wooster.]

The veteran TV presenter Anne Robinson, a fan of facelifts, gave one reason for her good looks as 'not eating crap food'. She believes Liverpool to be 'the glamour capital of Europe', and that legendary marble masterpiece from the Greek island of Milos is called the Venus dee Milo (rhymes with silo). No one says 'dee Gaulle' or 'Walter dee la Mere'. So why dee Milo rather than de (duh) Milo? Perhaps she just prefers it.

Are you expecting a 'dee-livery' or a dĕ-livery? Do you feel 'ree-jected'? Sure, there is such a word as 'ree-ject' (rēject, as a noun) but try not to say ree-jected (unless you want to be rĕjected, in better company!). Britain is 'the home of dĕmocracy' rather than 'the home of dē-mocracy'.

The BBC news presenter Chris Mason, whose accent strangely seems to have 'improved' in recent months, will talk of a 'ree-ward' rather than a rĕward. As for journalist Paul Mason, the committed socialist, it's painful to hear him mash all the vowels and consonants, usually into an endless 'postcapitalism' rant.

## The letter 'h'

I think it's best to say 'aitch'. If you say 'haitch' it sounds
pretty bad – in fact, it's usually a 'dead-give-away' of your
social class – despite what people might say to the con-
trary. Such as, 'Everyone says "haitch" these days' or 'You
can watch it in haitch-D.' If you said, 'MI-6 is my new
"haitch-queue"', not many people would believe you. The
World Health Organization, or WHO, is better as 'dou-
ble-U-aitch-O; don't say 'dubya-haitch-O' in an Oxbridge
interview, unless backed up by some seriously disadvantaged credentials likely to sway the university tutors.

Graham Norton came under fire from columnist Matthew Parris who likes taking pot-shots at public school
boys (from his grammar schoolboy and Cambridge-ed-
ucated perspective). Parris wrote in his column in *The
Times*,[4] 'I've listened again. He definitely said it. Graham
Norton said "haitch". All is lost.' Later he quotes from
Bernard Shaw's preface to *Pygmalion*: 'It is impossible for
the Englishman to open his mouth without making some
other Englishman hate or despise him.'

Mr Parris, an excellent journalist, has decided it's in
the best interests of everyone that 'privileged public school
boys' should always be 'sneered at', as this behaviour is
'healthy'. (It sounds to me a bit like a gripe from a grammar school boy.)

With the working classes, it's funny how they miss out
aitches when they shouldn't ('E got 'ammered last night)

and put them in when they shouldn't (e.g. 'the hegg in 'is 'and'). Wikipedia has a nice definition of 'aitch-dropping'. It's 'the deletion of the voiceless glottal fricative or "H sound"'. The reverse can also occur, which is known by linguists as 'H-insertion' or 'H-adding', also known as 'hypercorrection'. One of the most overworked quotes for hypercorrection (along with some spectacular 'aitch-dropping) is Eliza Doolittle's line in *My Fair lady*: 'In 'Ertford, 'Ereford and 'Ampshire 'urricanes 'ardly *hever* 'appen.' It's an attempt, self-consciously, to speak 'proper English'.

''E should get *hoff* 'is 'igh 'orse,' screamed the cockney cobbler in utter indignation.

(For the record, the French also have a habit of dropping their aitches. 'Vee 'ave zee 'abit of droppeeng our aitches, as you can see from watching '*Allo*, '*Allo*.')

For a short master class on 'simple phonetics, the science of speech', just listen to Rex Harrison (Audrey Hepburn played Eliza Doolittle) as Professor Higgins in the 1964 film, *My Fair Lady*.[5]

## The letter 's'

This is an odd one and mainly confined to young people. For some reason, they seem to prefer a kind of 'sh' beginning to some words beginning with an 's'. It should be a 'clean' 's'. Try saying 'student' (rhymes with stew) cleanly instead of 'shhtudent', 'strong' instead of shstrong. In America, however, you can get away with 'stoo-dent'. Sometimes Estuary English speakers will say 'shsstruggle' too.

It's not '*shtreet life*', as Miss Great Britain contestant Maria Ellinas was told by Simon Cowell in an *X Factor* audition. 'There's no "H" in the title of that song, "Street Life",' he told Ms Ellinas.

## The letter 't'

I am sure this is important despite the projections that we will all be speaking Estuary English by 2025. I have heard some Labour MPs say, 'Jeremy is not *parr* of the problem in the Labour party. He *is* the problem.' What is strange is that single syllable words seem to miss the final consonant (e.g. 'He loves sporr, and he loves to play his parr.') But, the same (Labour) MP may say 'bu-ut the Labour Party' correctly, and not say 'par-ee', missing out the 't' (a really bad sign!).

I don't yet understand how someone can say, 'It's really important (pronouncing the 't') but what we need is a strong pol-i-i-cal leader.'

Jeremy Corbyn, by the way, has an interesting debating style. At PMQs he is famous for reading out questions sent to him by his constituents, using their first names (Mavis, Janice, David, etc.). In debates, he will often speed up his delivery in the last few seconds, ending in a sort of petulant huff.

## The letter 'u'

Linguists could no doubt explain this much better; they have huge areas of expertise and can pronounce on the minutest detail. A BBC (or Sky News) commentator announces that 'Jessica Ennis has a consoomate (consummate) attention to detail.' (The old Received Pronunciation [RP] for consummate was 'con-SUM-at' but today it seems 'CON-syou-mut' or even 'CON-shoe-mut' has taken over.) This is fairly rare but much more common is the dreaded 'assume', which gets bastardised to 'ashoom', mainly by cockneys and Londoners, especially those from Essex. It seems to be too hard for them to say 'ass-youm'. Now, *ass-shooming* you follow me, there are some other words where the pronunciation of 'u' is often an either/ or situation. Some Scots say they will 'syou' the pants off someone, but mostly 'soo' is preferred, with 's-you' or 'syou' sounding affected, as it would be if you said 'syou-pernatural' rather than soopernatural. 'Just inform your syou-periors that I want my bottles back,' said Mrs Hyacinth Bucket to the milkman in one (*Keeping Up Appearances*) episode. *Note:* another incongruous variation for 'ass-youm' (preferred) is 'ass-soom'. It's fine if you are in the US, though. It's the American pronunciation.

No doubt you'd be laughed at for saying '*syou-per*' rather than *sooper* (super). Nevertheless, lots of people would say 'I'm going to SYOU/SEUW the pants off Goldman Sachs' while others say 'they will SOO (sue) Goldman Sachs'. And if you wanted to pursue the case further in court, do you per-soo it or per-syou it? To be honest, I don't think one should per-soo anything unless you are American!

Angela Rayner MP likes to say that she is 'per-shoo-in' the matter further'. Whatever, please also say 'doo-vays' for duvets and not dyou/dewvays.

A few people still talk about what they have in their 'syout-cases' but this is no better than a Mrs Bucket bossing her syou-periors. A soootcase seems best to me, whether you are in Hampstead or Harrogate (or 'Ampstead or 'Arrogate). Old style RP pronunciation of 'pollution' was 'poll-you-shn' but now it's 'poll-oo-shn', just as 'rac-see-al' was old RP for racial (ray-shl).

Lord Lexden (Alistair Cooke), giving a speech (chaired by Speaker John Bercow) on Anthony Eden's life as a conservative prime minister, being of the 'old guard' of course, referred to the 'Syou-ez' Canal seized by President Nässer (not Nässer). Today, for nearly everyone, unless they are octogenarian ladies-in-waiting to the Queen or crusty old colonels frequenting a London gentleman's club, it's the 'Soo-ez' (Suez) Canal and President Nässer. You could break this down further into 'Soo-iz' (old RP) and 'Soo-ez', but never mind.

Welsh speakers, such as Neil Kinnock, former leader of the Labour Party, have problems with the letter 'u' in words like constituency. Instead of the usual 'constit*you*ency' it comes out as 'constit-u-ency' (that's 'consti-ooo-ency'). Many Labour politicians prefer to talk about the NRC (National Executive Committee) as 'the exec-i-tive', neatly missing out the 'u'. They also, in the main, have ad'erents (*a-dear-ents*) instead of adherents (but that's an 'h' problem).

Hearing about 'consoomer noos' (consumer news) is another bugbear (sometimes you'll hear 'con-shoomer', which is worse). Do you like 'noo-trients' in your breakfast cereal or 'new-trients'? "E told me 'e noo abou' i' coz e'd 'erd i' on the noos.' It's entirely possible to hear a sentence like this in many cities and towns in the UK. Actually, Professor Brian Cox on his TV programmes talks of black holes *consooming* (consuming) vast amounts of matter (but the writer is more than happy to add, 'Who cares!' Brian Cox is surely way above any petty criticism. He is a great man and a great scientist.)

As there is a 'u' in 'issue', there's just time to mention, David Cameron talks of 'ishues' but Jeremy Corbyn likes 'iss-yous' [that is, he did, as the last time I heard him, he was talking about 'isshues'.] Why is this? Iss-you, I think, is a little bit affected too, like the syoupernatural for supernatural above, but in another way. An ishoo/iss-shoe is preferable.

I'm sure some 'pronunciation perfectionists' also like to say how much they 'appree-see-ate' things. Do you appree-shee-ate or appree-see-ate? I prefer the former, as the latter is much too affected to stand up to proper scrutiny. I know some people like to say 'appree-see-ate' but Lord Soames, as far as I know, is not one of them, and I'm content to follow his lead, especially when one knows what he likes for breakfast.

Jeremy Corbyn likes to 'enthoose' about things rather than 'enthyous'. It makes me less than *enthoosiastic* (enthusiastic)! John McDonnell, Shadow Chancellor of the

Exchequer, wants the Bank of England 'to ex-ood (exude) confidence about the economy' (whilst 'ending this government's austerity programme, which has ruined lives up and down the country ... and we will throw light on where the tax dodgers are hiding their money ... Under Labour, there'll be *no more Philip Greens* at all.' [Green's alma mater: Carmel College, nicknamed the 'Jewish Eton', where he was a boarder until aged 15.] Under the next Labour government, 'everyone will earn enough to live on'. 'No one will be left behind.' Good. I won't have to keep looking in the reduced aisle in Waitrose.)

Just to complete the picture, the octogenarian Labour MP David Winnick, whose intellect is still razor-sharp, rounded on Sir Philip in the House of Commons (20 October 2016), describing him as 'a billionaire spiv who should never have received a knighthood'. The 'spiv' finally sold ailing BHS to a thrice-bankrupt for a pound.

A peculiar question. Is it 'lever-idge' (sounds like school leaver) or 'lever-idge' (sounds like leveret – a young hare under one year)? Philip Hammond, the new Tory Chancellor of the Exchequer likes to say 'leverage' with the latter pronunciation (American English) but British English uses the good old 'lever' style.

As for the way 'chancellor' is pronounced perhaps we can leave that to one side for now – but it doesn't (in my little book) rhyme with chandelier!

## Eeether or Eyether?

When my daughter asked me, was it *eye*-ther or *ee*-ther, I replied, 'Both are correct but eyether (either) is better.' Neether (neither) always seemed less fine than nyether (neither); neether was always a bit sneakier and slightly underhand and 'nyether' was definitely better.

## Pronouncing English words like the Americans

In the US, they have their ways of saying things, like the bonnet of a car is the hood, and a tap, that humble device, is a 'faucet'. They say 'swăthe' to rhyme with wrath but we say swāthe, to rhyme with lathe. Do you like prīvacy in the băthroom? We English do say prīvate, but it's prĭvacy, not prīvacy, as more than once I had to remind my children. There are dozens of other examples, too many to list here, including saying 'ad-verTYSEment' instead of 'AD-VER-TISS-ment.

Americans love to say 'Eyerăq' rather than Irāq (or Irăq), 'Eyeran' for Iran, and they also figyurr things out instead of figuring them (out).

A child with asthma (as-mah) has 'az-ma' in the US. The use of a 'z' sometimes creeps in to eccentric English pronunciations, like 'ab-zurd' for 'ab-surd'. In the same way, some people talk about 'pezzi-mism' instead of 'pessi-mism', and post Brexit (what a lovely clean sound there is in 'exit'), we have to put up with Faisal Islam (and

Andrew Neil of Sunday Politics, who incidentally likes to pronounce Jean-Paul Sartre as in 'SATT-RUH') on the BBC talking about 'Breggs-zit'. It's adding eggs to injury. What is wrong with 'Brex-it'? It says 'EXIT' on the door, not 'EGGSIT', doesn't it? (Faisal Islam is a British journalist of Bengali Indian ethnicity. Alma mater: Manchester Grammar School, Trinity College, Cambridge, and City University, London.) And Faisal does say 'eggsit' too! I heard it tonight.☺ He also likes 'äftă-dinner coffee' but, as we are going to learn later, this is because of the 'Trap–Bath split' (see p. 167–68).

In the US, it's all about 'doo-ty', as opposed to 'dew-ty'. They like YŌ-guerrt rather than yoghurt. They walk on 'sidewalks', we walk on 'pavements'.

Like Van Gogh (Goff) and his paintings? In the US, they talk of 'Van Go'. 'Skedule' instead of schedule (*shed-yul*) is commonly mis-pronounced by British speakers too. As for tights, in the US they go by the faintly seedy name of 'pantyhose'. With the word 'luxury', it sounds like the Americans are *lugging* this heavy word around with them! It comes out as '*luggs-sury*', completely unlike our cleaner sounding lux-ury. (For an extensive list of British English/American English see www.WhichEnglish.com.[6])

It's strange how a word like 'gonna' for 'going to', originally from the US and seen as 'a bit sloppy' for an RP person, has gone mainstream. Now, every last cabinet minister, of whichever political party, is happy to talk about all the changes their party is 'gonna' make. It was a favourite of George Osborne's. Gotta for 'got to' is also prevalent. 'We've gotta recognise (*reconise*) we're 14 points behind the Tories.'

## English howlers

Here are three you can try to avoid. Lots of people think that things 'esculate' but really they escalate. 'It was just *esculating* all the time I had the coffee *perculator* going.' Things esc*a*late, and coffee pots perc*o*late. These are just three examples of 'howlers', albeit minor. *'The esculating athalete got stuck in the coffee perculator.'* (Please don't ask why the athlete became lodged in the percolator.)

The Olympic Games have their fair share of athletes but often you will hear something like (this is another cockney/London aberration), 'Britain needs first-class "athaletes" in order to compete against the world.' Listen carefully. 'Ath-a-leets'. An athlete is an *ath-lete*. Period. Not an ath-a-leet/ath-a-lete!

Some presenters will say an athlete has just won a 'med-aw' instead of making it 'medal'. 'Mo Farah has got gold! It's a gold *med-aw* for Mo.'

Why do sports presenters have to present themselves (usually) as slightly more 'thick' than the average TV presenter? Take a very small word – if you say this wrong, you will give the appearance of being a little bit stupid. It is not 'lit-all', never mind about 'li'all'. I mean where there is a sad effort to pronounce the 't' as if it must be included in the pronunciation to sound right. Actually, in this case it's two syllables, but sounds a bit like 'baby talk'. 'The "litt-tall" boy felt very upset when his mother locked him in his bedroom.' Try to say little slightly 'clipped', with the emphasis on the *li*', not two equal length syllables as in 'lit-tall'. Incidentally, in British television, there are two occasions, possibly three, when an introductory gleeful smile is de rigueur from presenters – when announcing that 'sport' is up next or even better, 'it's time to catch up on the weather'. *'Let's see what the weather has got in store!'* The third obligatory occasion is the birth of a royal baby.

Cockneys and London taxi drivers, are they part of this world? No, for them, the word 'world' has to be pronounced as something like 'weld'. 'The richest man in the weld,' you can hear if you listen carefully. It's not world, to rhyme with whirled, however they say it. Cockney cyclists ride on 'bykes', sounds a bit like boike, whereas you should aim to ride (sounds like) a bike. Another favourite of 'Romford Man', as well as pronouncing 'world' uniquely is the simple word, 'year'. Ideally, it has but one syllable. I prefer 'yer' but this isn't the choice of everyone. Note to Reader: In fact Romford man is neither Cockney nor Essex man, as Romford is now part of Greater London. I had a good friend who grew up there but that was seventy years ago. For the true Romford, Essex man it's a YEE-AH. As in, 'Oi've bin goin' dahn the Old Kent Road for yee-ahs and yee-ahs and yee-ahs.' Cockneys are also fond of the double negative in speech, e.g. 'I don't know nuffink.'

Cockneys are prone to address males of higher rank, as a mark of respect, as 'Guv' or governor.

It must be really difficult if you are a foreign tourist who speaks very little English – you're in a London pub trying a pint of ale. Hesitantly, you ask the man near you, 'Excuse me sir, where is the toilet/loo?' The man with the hangdog expression hardly seems to notice, but answers with a nod of his head to a man going down some stairs, '*Follow that geezah* (geezer), *dahn the apples 'n' pears.*'

## A few bêtes noires

Why do Scottish presenters have to say the number 'thirteen' as 'thirt-teen'? God knows. I suppose one must be careful about criticising the Welsh, too. The 'lilt' they have acquired over hundreds if not thousands of years – when speaking in English – is unique but it can be a little 'teee-di-us' to have to 'lis-sunn' to it all the time.

In the south of England any name of a county ending in '-shire' is usually pronounced as, say, Oxford-sheer'. BBC news presenter Julian Worricker likes to remind viewers they can catch up later with Victoria Derby-sheer. I think it's better to say 'Oxford-shir' and 'Derby-shir', certainly not 'shire', to rhyme with mire, equally not 'sheer' to rhyme with 'weir'. Derbyshir, Oxfordshir, Hamshir (to rhyme with whirr) instead of Derby-sheer, Oxford-sheer, and 'Hamp-sheer'. If you say, 'I am in Hamp-sheer for the weekend', it might mark you out as, how shall we say, a little provincial?

A similar 'gripe' is the pronunciation of health. Again in the south of England, to a casual listener it sounds like '*halth*', as in 'The nation's halth is really important.' Why not say it as it really is, 'hellth'?

And another *gripe*. Why do some people say '*medjeval*' rather than 'med-ee-val' or 'medi-evil'? Try listening. (It might have something to do with the variant spelling, mediaeval.) Others like 'abzurd' for absurd and 'Dezember' for December. Why, I don't know. Even a simple word like 'because' can be pronounced *be-cāwse*, *bec☒z*, or *bec☒z*.

One extraordinary pronunciation was a word spoken by Chris Packham on a TV programme on animals. Something or someone had 'renn-*aged*' on their part of the deal (it's reneged, with a hard 'g'). One BBC news presenter, commenting on the Oscar Pistorius trial, declared confidently that the accused 'had been found guilty of culpable *homo*cide' (as in *hoe*-mo-cide – a frightening prospect involving hoes or whores). The *hom* in homicide is preferable with a short 'o' (rhymes with bomb or Herbert Lom).

By the way, please don't say you like to get 'invōlved' (rhymes with holed). Do say 'invŏlved', with the 'o' sound as in holly. Another bête noire has to be interviewees on TV, especially from large organisations, 'mechanically' starting every sentence with, 'So...' (I have to thank an exceptional reader who has explained why. 'The proper use of this sort of joining word [so] is 'well'. The use of 'so' is really for continuing a conversation where one is explaining what happened next. 'So then I did...'.)

# Names that confuse – personal names and place names with 'counterintuitive pronunciations' – not ones you can guess from their spellings

If taken out somewhere grand, like Harry's Bar in London's Mayfair, not that they would probably stock this item, be sure not to ask for *Cock*burn's Port. Ask for Co-burn's.

I once met a man on a train from Bournemouth to London. He announced himself as 'The next Lord Bister' (rhymes with sister). As I was then only 18, I imagined there was a place called 'Bister' and later found out he would have written this as 'The next Lord Bicester'.

If in Leicester (Lesster) visiting the stately home of Belvoir Castle, seat of the Dukes of Rutland, don't be fooled by the French looking name. It's pronounced exactly the same as the rodent that uses timber to create its own home – the beaver.

In blessed Oxford town, near the Botanical Gardens, you might be paying a visit to Magdalen College, motto *Floreat Magdalena*, founded in 1458. Note no final 'e'. However, its odd pronunciation is world famous. It's the same as being in that tearfully sentimental state, usually after one too many – maudlin (mawd-lin). Its sister college in Cambridge, Magdalene College, whose name was given an extra 'e' in the 19th century to avoid confusion with Oxford by the GPO, the General Post Office, is commonly supposed to be pronounced as 'Magdalen(e)' but this is a popular misconception. Both colleges are traditionally pronounced as '*mawd-lin*'. For a long time, ever since someone told me, a bit like a proud know-it-all, that 'it's "maudlin", you know, in Oxford but Magdalene in Cambridge', I had repeated the same mistake. For Wikipedia's alerting me to this, I shall always have a good word to say for co-founder Jimmy Wales, whatever his critics say.

The Lascelles family (cousins of the Queen) takes the pronunciation 'Lassels' and not Lass-cells. Here are just a few other famous names from dozens if not hundreds that can stump foreigners as well as natives – or the other way round.

| | |
|---|---|
| Beauchamp | beecham |
| Beaufoy | boffy |
| Blount | blunt |
| Beaulieu | byoo-lee |
| Cecil | sissle |
| Cadogan | ca'duggan |
| Cholmondeley | chumley |
| Cowper | cooper |
| Crichton | cryton |
| John Donne | dunn |
| Eyre | air |
| Featherstonehaugh | fanshaw |
| Fotheringay | fungey |
| Ralph Fiennes | raif fines |
| Grosvenor | grow-v'ner |

| | |
|---|---|
| Home *or* Hulme | hewm |
| John Maynard Keynes | kānes *but* Milton Keynes ('keens') |
| Keats | keets |
| Mainwaring | man-er-ring |
| Marjoribanks | marchbanks |
| McGillycuddy | mac-li-cuddy |
| Menzies | ming-is |
| Melhuish | mell-ish |
| Nighy | nye |
| Pomfret | pum-fret |
| Sandys | sands |
| St Clair | sin-clair |
| St John | sin-jun |
| Urquhart | erk-urt |
| Wolseley | wools-ly |
| Worcester | wooster |
| Yeats | yates |

I suppose it's fair to say the average person is not going to meet up with all of this very short selection of names very often, if it all, if ever. One should at least get the poets right, like Yeats and Donne (shame on you if you don't know how to say *Seamus* Heaney), and knowing how to pronounce the name of economist John Maynard Keynes is essential in a viva voce (*veeva vochay*) (often shortened to 'viva') examination in economic theory – where you give a verbal defence of your written thesis. Beyond that, it's hardly of any consequence to know that Mr Beaufoy is Mr Boffy or that Mr Fotheringay be addressed as Mr Fungey.

A great old oak stood in my school grounds until hooligans finally burnt it to cinders. The immense old tree was known as 'the Mountjoy oak' but it was pronounced by the cognoscenti, both young and old, as 'mungee' (soft 'g'). Old Mungy is no more but lives on in the school's collective memory.

# CHAPTER THREE

*Miss Annie Ting – an Irish yarn (poor old Fido) – Rick Stein's pistachios – Victor Meldrew's gooseberries – Kingsley Amis sounds off – guns over Kimmeridge Bay – more odd or different pronunciations*

Funny 'ting' about the Irish, is it not? We go to see a film, they go to a 'fil-lumm' or 'fillum'. They do love their 'turra-breds' at the races. But the Irish, well, that's another story. Have you heard of *Annie Ting*? That's the way the Irish pronounce 'anything'!

(If it is not out of place, perhaps I can add a story from an Irishman. He was a stout fellow, tall, with a red-veined face and a fat stomach. He'd sit for hours in the same place, drinking his way through ten pints in a day, regaling his friends (and others who couldn't help listening) to story after story, for hour upon hour. He loved his jokes. I remember one. It was when he was growing up in Ireland, when there was no food to eat, they were so poor. They would eat shoe leather just to survive. One day, it was decided that their dog, Fido, had to be sacrificed (those weren't his words) to feed the family. They were starving, so Fido ended up on the table for dinner in a big pot. All the family, including the grandmother were weeping at the thought of poor old Fido, having been 'taken'. But they had to eat some'ting. When they were all licking their lips a little later in the evening, taking away the plates, the grandmother turned to her son, saying. 'T'is a pity poor Fido wasn't here to enjoy that dinner. He would have loved them bones!')

## Rick Stein cooks up some pistachios

To return to England and Rick Stein in one of his food programmes; he was talking about a nut (actually a drupe) near to my heart – pistachio nuts. The reason why I love these healthy nuts is solely because I was fortunate enough to be introduced to them by the woman I later married. She comes from Iran and Iranians love eating them. They call them '*pist-tash*'.

Whether someone uses a long or short 'a' in words is really none of anyone's business but, being a southerner by birth, I can't help preferring a pāssport to a păssport, a grāph to a grăph, and a bāth to a băth so I was slightly surprised when I heard Rick Stein refer to a recipe and the 'pistachios' he used (with a long 'a' vowel sound, like the sound one makes when a doctor gets you to open your mouth and say 'aaah'). 'No, Rick,' I felt like saying, 'they're pistăchios (the -ach rhyming with just that – ash – what you get when burning something like wood).

Anyway, Rick calls them pistāchios.

## Mr Meldrew's guz-bumps

This led me to consider other vowels and the first person (I can't believe it!) to fall into my 'vowel-trap' was the actor Richard Wilson (as Victor Meldrew). 'Yes,' he said, 'I was watching this person on TV, and can you beleeeve it, it gave me *guz-bumps*.'

Immediately, I could not fail to notice the unusual nature of the pronunciation but I suppose there are plenty of people who talk of guz-berries and guz-bumps instead of gooseberries and goose bumps. (I might add, as an oddity, that in Iranian or Farsi 'guz' is something unpleasant. If a Muslim emits a *gŭz* [fart] when washing in preparation for prayer, he or she must begin the ritual all over again.) It's true what they say about famous last words. No sooner written, then up crops Hugh Fearnley-Whittingstall at his Dorset cottage retreat and he mentions harvesting 'guz-berries'. EmmaSaying calls them 'goooze-berries'. No sign of the 's' in goose.

This takes me back to schooldays when my ginger-haired Latin master excoriated me for saying forehead (when it should have been *forred*') and toothbrush (when I should have said '*tuthbrush*'). Happily these silly distinctions are all but gone today but you can still hear faint echoes of this earlier form of received pronunciation with words like room (*rŭm*) (rhymes with 'cogito, ergo *sum*'). Another word is 'problem', which for the landed gentry or aristocracy, judges or the like, has the habit of sounding like 'prob-lim'. 'It was not really a prob-lim, you know.' Novelist Kingsley Amis was certain that an English RP speaker 'worth his salt' had to pronounce 'always' as AWLwhizz.[1]

Similarly with words like 'constable' (cun-sta-ble). In America, they call the men in blue the 'PO-lease' (police) whereas the old RP pronunciation around the fringes of Scotland Yard and from Tory politicians at police conferences ('cun-fren-ces) is more like 'plis' or 'plys', as in 'Our PLYS must deal with crime on the doorstep.' Boris Johnson may pronounce 'perhaps' as *praps*, *phaps* or *paps* (sounds like). (For an astute observation of 'police vernacular', please see the penultimate quatrain in John Betjeman's poem, 'The Arrest of Oscar Wilde at the Cadogan Hotel'.[2])

I find myself hesitating. Mostly the sound of hesitation in speech is either *um* (to rhyme with thumb), *er* (in the military especially, also politicians, to rhyme with her) and *erm* in Liverpool (to rhyme with, well it's not easy to find a word that rhymes with the uniquely Liverpudlian *erm*). The military *er* can also be written as '*ur*'; *er* or *ur* pauses allow time for the military man's mental thinking whilst speaking aloud, otherwise known as thinking on one's feet.

## Guns off Kimmeridge Bay

One old general, wheeled into the TV studio, dispensed with any dithering when asked whether soldiers in the British Army were under-equipped for warfare in Iraq. He leaned forward, bellowing without hesitation, 'SQUADDIE needs BOOTS!'

(I was once fossil hunting near Kimmeridge, and thinking that more fossils might be found at the far end of the beach, wandered off in that direction, having failed to notice the red flag flying on a pole to warn Ministry of Defence (MOD) firing was in progress. Suddenly, an imposing figure in army uniform appeared on the cliff top, glaring down at me. 'Get away from there,' he shouted. 'Can't you read? Move back!' He waved his arms towards the near end of the beach.

Having picked up earlier on the use of the word 'squaddie', I shouted into the wind, 'Is that an order, SQUADDIE?' 'Yes Sir,' he bellowed back, 'Now get off that effing part of the beach. NOW!') A 'squaddie' is an archaic term for an Indian irregular soldier seconded to the British Army in India. Nowadays it just means a private soldier. There is nothing about pronunciation here, just the faintly patronising air of a word used to describe 'a common or garden' soldier. Since I was in all probability being sworn at by a private and not a general, I couldn't resist trying it out.

Apologies for this perhaps appearing to be one shibboleth after another but have you noticed how Labour Party members always have comrades or 'friends' whereas the Tories seem to have more colleagues? One is tempted to say 'Who needs enemies with friends like these' – with reference to Boris Johnson and Michael Gove or Jeremy Corbyn and Tom Watson.

## More odd or different pronunciations

After all these tribulations I am feeling as if a head massage might soothe away all the mental aches and pains – but then I remember another peculiar English pronunciation, one commonly used by Londoners from somewhere like Romford in Essex (*correction: Romford was in Essex, now it forms part of the London borough of Havering in Greater London*) and/or Cockneys. Instead of a mass*euse* (to rhyme with the River Meuse if you are French) the word is corrupted to 'mass-*suse*', the latter half of the word rhyming with the Greek father of the gods, Zeus. Brainbox Danny Baker says 'sabatoyers' for saboteurs; the Americans tend to say 'entreprenoyers' too.

Do you say 'am-a-chur' or 'am-a-ter' (amateur)? Is it a scallop or a scollop? It's a scallop (rhymes with pallet) but most British people seem to think it's a scollop (rhymes with dollop). One thing I'm certain about is that a hybrid does have an 'h' in front of it, despite the TV adverts that horribly bastardise the word, presumably to sound more authentic to the working man. 'The new 4 x 4 ''ybrid' – 'eyebrid' or ''ibrid', drones the nasty-sounding man.

Another advert asks, 'Is there any veneer in 'ere?' ad infinitum, knocking on any old piece of wood to see if there's any veneer (in there), priding itself on a clever little rhyme, no better than the supposedly shortest poem, which is:

*Adam*
*Had 'em.*

Of course, surprise, surprise! The veneer advert was later banned by the Advertising Standards Authority. The 'solid hardwood' was made from pieces of hardwood glued together, then covered with an 'oak wrap', and the wrap was in effect a veneer. So, 'No veneer in 'ere' was a fib.

Another, 'simply dreadful' (I can imagine Joanna Lumley saying that) advert concerned a household cleaner of sinks and plugholes, something similar to *Cillit Bang*, which is tipped into a plughole to clean it. [For those who are dyslexic be careful how you pronounce *Cillit Bang* – it's pronounced 'sillit bang', with a soft 'c'.] A BBC magazine article describes the name as sounding '…like the alter ego of a bassist in a Turkish punk band or an ineligible Scrabble contribution'.) 'Poh-oles' is also becomming common for 'potholes'.

The advert's ending line for this new plughole cleaner is: 'Plug'oles need love too.' Despair: *I just don't want to live in a world with 'plug'oles an' 'ibrids'!* Do you?

# CHAPTER FOUR

*This 'correction malarkey' – my friend gets 'mizled' – more difficult words for non-native speakers – the wonder of everyday accents – Mr Eric Pickles MP on Desert Island Discs – Si qua est et gloria (If there is any glory in this…)*

S OMETIMES ONE NEEDS TO take a break from all this 'correction malarkey'. It can become a little tedious. To lighten the job a little, may I suggest pretending for a moment you are Welsh. You say to yourself, *teee-deee-uss*, putting in a crisp, upward lilt in the middle. It may bring a tiny wry smile. That's by way of a humorous respite. How *do* you say that word? It seems to be (British English) either res-PYTE or RES-pyte, and American English RESS-PIT (i.e. equal stress on the last one).

Talking of wry, a friend of mine when a boy was convinced that the correct way to say awry (ă-rye) was awe-ree. He said people looked at him a little *awe-ree* when he mentioned the word. If he saw the word 'misled' he did not see it is 'mis-led', as in taking wrong advice, but 'misled', to rhyme with aisle(d), pronounced mizled. He said he preferred to talk about having been 'mizled' (i.e. misled) because 'mizled', he thought, sounded better than 'miss-led' as it was more tragic (like being burgled!). If things went wrong at school, he could complain to his mother (to gain sympathy): '*But Mama, I've been mizled!*'

## Some difficult words for non-native speakers

The last thing I wish to do is to write a small book with lists of words that successful people never say. One thing highly successful people DON'T do every day is to look up lists of things highly successful people DO every day. I have read that one of the most difficult words to pronounce is the name for a narrow strip of land with sea on either side – an *isthmus* (rhymes with Christmas), as in the obscure doggerel:

> *I spent Christmas*
> *On an isthmus*
> *With nothing better to do.*

People who have not been in this country for too long often seem to mispronounce the same words. In a discussion about Israelis and Palestinians, you often hear 'Israeli' (rhymes somewhat with Disraeli) pronounced as 'Is-ray-*eel*-ee' but this is no doubt correct in the country of origin. Then there may be discussion of 'bomb-*bing*', perhaps a mistake anyone could make as one would not know the second 'b' in 'bombing' is silent. 'Against' is often again-est or a-gen-est (hard 'g').

Many Indians and Pakistanis have difficulty with 'v' and 'w' so you might hear, '*No, vee are not beleewing in that.*' A regime is pronounced sometimes as 'ray-geem' with a hard 'g' rather than a soft one, a mistake also made by some TV presenters. However, this is an entirely different subject not to be taken further. I have tried to pronounce the Qur'an (Koran) in the correct way as pronounced by Muslims or Arabs, and truly it is quite difficult.

British people anyway have problems of their own – in their own language. One interviewee on TV, when asked about the money paid to Europe every year by Britain, replied. 'It's *astromical*, init?' Another, when asked what Britain ought to do, stay in Europe or leave, replied: 'Nah, we should leave straightaway *and get Britain back to where it is.*'

In some far-fetched stretch of the imagination, this is not so distant from T.S. Eliot's, 'In my end is my beginning', if you can get back to where you are now, having left...

## The wonder of everyday accents

If anyone should think I am against accents and dialects, unless they conform to my own personal preferences, think again! Enter any pub or bar, the length and breadth of the country and you'll find wonderfully rich accents, imbued with history, depth, locality. If you could stand in these places, unnoticed like the invisible man, and *just listen*, you'll hear the wonder, richness and beauty, the character of all the characters on the greatest stage of all – everyday life in everyday places. This could be anywhere in Britain –

from Ireland to Scotland to Wales to a Dorset inn or a Cornish fishing village.

It can be a pleasure to listen to Sir Eric Jack Pickles MP (alma mater: Leeds Metropolitan University), a former conservative party chairman. He doesn't have the carefully moderated tones of the late Roy Plomley (pronounced plum-ley), who used to host *Desert Island Discs*. (You can listen to Eric Pickles's voice by following this link.[1]) Eric Pickles wouldn't be the same without his rich accent that makes a larger than life character even larger. He's the kind of man you wouldn't expect to be a progressive 'One Nation' Tory with his 'man of the people' mien.

He was born into a family that had always supported Labour, and as a youngster admits to having been hugely sympathetic towards communism. At the age of 16, angered by the Soviet Union's brazen invasion of Czechoslovakia, he joined the Young Conservatives.

Mr Pickles happens to be a flag enthusiast, and is from Keighley in West Yorkshire. How boring it would be if we all spoke in the same way. So it's fair to say that life thrives on accents, dialects and little differences, eccentricities and quirks; we are the more human for them. (Another politician born in Keighley is the Labour MP and former shadow chancellor of the exchequer, Chris Leslie; a man always happy to extol the merits of the Labour party, more often than not with a passing dig at the Tories.)

Sir Eric Pickles, by the way, has a wry sense of humour too. In a select committee hearing looking at anti-Semitism in the Labour Party, he remarked that in the civil service the definition of anti-Semitism some years back was 'being more unreasonable than is usual to a Jew'. The discussion had touched on Ed Milliband being Jewish, and a few moments later, when asked if he were saying that anti-Semitism had been completely curtailed in the Conservative Party, he remarked, 'No, I am not saying that, not for one hundredth of a *milli*-second – no pun intended…'

Instead, perhaps ponder the paucity of articulation in modern English and how being stumped by disadvantage, by lack of meaningful education, stymies so many young people. You can hear the word 'like' repeated like an endless clichéd mantra, but it explains little and gives even less clarity or vision. In a supermarket aisle are three girls shopping for lunch; one breaks away from the others, saying, 'I'm just going like to get some sparkling water like. You know, not just water like, but, like, sparkling water like.' It is needless poverty of expression too, not just paucity of articulation.

After such a sweeping view of British life, I am wondering what niche to get into next. Were I in the US, I would hear Americans talk of 'nitt-chez'. They clearly don't like niches (neesh-es). How about these very minor niches? Mark Urban, a rather good political commentator at the BBC talks of 'enemy sträff-ing' rather than sträfing (although at other times he might say sträfing) (to rhyme with Raif) and Rachel Johnson (sister to Boris) is so very keen on 'I just "hat" to answer that' (quite common), rather than 'had to'. (The Americans talk of 'Cōasta Rica' rather than Cŏsta Rica. Is it pitta (or pita) bread (sounds like Peter) or pit-ta bread? Am I in peat or a pit?

Sometimes the only answer is to find a quote to 'get out of jail'. 'Like one who stands on a far-off promontory, and spies a far-off land' – where escape might lie.

According to John Humphreys in his book *Lost for Words*,[2] 'The battle for pronunciation will never be won or lost – although it's really more a light skirmish than a fight to the death. What matters more than how we speak is what we say.'

To grab a leaf out of Virgil and Boris Johnson (one of his recent *obiter dicta*): '*Si qua est ea gloria...*' (If there is any glory in this...'), I will choose a quote from the 1953 film, *Shane*. I might change it slightly.

The original quote: 'A man has to be what he is. There's no breaking the mould...There's no going back.'

How about this? 'A man has to say what he says. There's no breaking the mould... There's no going back.'

# CHAPTER FIVE

*The dastardly perpetrators! Bring them to justice!*
*Burglars and coupons – using déclassé in conversations –*
*plumping for Occam's razor – words of four or more*
*syllables – gender – some TV shows – crafting on TV –*
*play Sudoku for ever!*

ONE OF THE ODDITIES of the English language is that
no one can find a better word for someone who does
something dastardly than 'the perpetrator'. The word has a
mid-16th century origin, meaning something 'performed to
completion'. In the original Latin, it could be either good
or bad. In England, it was used in legal statutes to refer to
something bad, and hence negative.

It has an oddly sinister ring. *'Catch the perpetrators!*
*Hold them to account! Bring them to justice!'* Perpetrators
have to do something horrible, a crime such as capturing
Yazidi women to be used as slaves. That's 'Dash' for you,
as United States Secretary of State John Kerry likes to call
them (normally pronounced Da-esh). Perhaps, after all,
we need a word like 'perpetrator'. It might have sublimi-
nal associations with 'traitors'. No one is going to accuse a

person who has overstayed a parking bay as 'a perpetrator', so perhaps further discussion is not appropriate.

If you happen to be a West African living in a remote rural area though, where Pidgin English is still spoken, a 'dash' is a gift but I don't suppose anyone will tell Secretary Kerry it's 'Daesh' and not 'Dash'.

## Burglars and coupons

Back on the shores of Britain and once the football season gets underway, the name of Wembley is on everyone's lips. I think the name, correctly, is pronounced 'Wem-blee' but the word often emerges with three syllables rather than two. It becomes 'Wem-be-ley', and pronounced like this it's really more suited to the Wombles of Wimbledon. *To be honest*, it takes a slight effort, as least for me, to stick to two syllables and not get lazy and use three – that's 'tree' if you're Irish. A similar thing happens when visiting Audley Street in Mayfair, which is Aud-ley but which on occasion sounds more like 'orderly'. A similar effect is found when children start reading books about a bur-gal-ar, like *Burglar Bill*. It takes a while to stop saying bur-gar-lar (?) and instead say 'bur-glur' (burgler).

If you walk up to Oxford Street from Audley Street, someone might offer you a coupon – a 'coo-pon'. I don't know why this is but some people insist that it's a 'kew-pon' (heard on Channel 4's *Breakfast Brunch*) (rather like an esoteric gift from Kew Gardens). Another guest, asked to choose between various kinds of tea, replied, 'Aesthetically, I'm gonna go for that', except that aesthetically it didn't sound right because she said 'Ass-thetically'.

The sound '*aes*' is not pronounced '*asc*' but as '*ees*-thetically. Most users of the word have probably never distinguished between an ascetic and an aesthete.

## Using déclassé in conversations

The various subtle gradations in pronunciation have been altering for decades, even centuries because language is always changing, assimilating new words, modifying accents. With words, it's true to say you *can* teach an old dog new tricks. Listening to *Made in Chelsea*'s Louise Thompson (well I think it was her), I heard a word you don't hear much on everyday chat shows. She dismissed something or other as déclassé, something that has fallen in social status. Despite having worked with words for most of my life, I can't remember ever having noticed déclassé or, *to be honest*, ever having used it in conversation.

It's quite a useful word. Much conversation has clearly gone déclassé – here's one small example. Another chat show guest described her excitement at a new discovery: '*Shi-h*', she said solemnly, '*i' is qui'e excitin'.*'

The girl (Louise Thompson) did know something because not much later I think she used the word 'Elysium' to announce a state of great happiness, although in Greek mythology the Elysian Fields were somewhere the heroes went after death. Only problem is that she pronounced it '*Elee*-see-i-um' – but then I realised she might have been influenced by an American boyfriend, or was a Brit who had spent some time in America, so it was fine! She hadn't gone déclassé at all.

It occurred to me later that rather than idle speculation as to how this might have happened, it was a fine choice to plump for Occam's razor (the principle of making no more assumptions than necessary). So, I'd settle for her picking this up on an American visit.

Before celebrating, this unique fact, however, a rule of thumb used to be that the lower class(es) (that's the socially and economically disadvantaged) often had problems when faced with pronouncing words of *four or more syllables*. A famous example of a longish word stumping (in this case) a socially advantaged person was the umpire in a Martina Navratilova tennis match. He was eventually met with laughter and derision when making a truly stuttering delivery of her surname: 'Nav-ra-til-ov-a'. But perhaps the four-syllable 'rule' needs updating. A lot of people (or a lorra people, e.g. Cilla Black, Cheryl Cole) use a three-syllable word to express their admiration for something by saying, '*It's qual-i-ee, mate. Qual-i-ee.*'

As a footnote to how fast things change in life (and not just words), a newsflash just came up. 'Uber launches self-driving taxis.' The robots are coming.

## Gender

It's not fair to bring gender into the argument for better pronunciation. I was going to say that men and women are just the same, except that men swear more. But, there's a long list of female stars who also swear like navvies, sailors or troopers.

In the list (to name only a very few) are Keira Knightley, Sarah Millican (when she's in a bad mood), Dame Helen Mirren, Katherine Ryan (an Irish Canadian, which *perhaps* explains something), Sheridan Smith, Ruby Wax, Kate Winslet, and the pioneering comedian Joan Rivers, who had the bad luck to meet the wrong surgeon – for a minor throat procedure in Manhattan.

If you seriously want to hear some choice female accents in one place, there are few better places to start than with the likeable Joseph Patrick 'Paddy' McGuinness and his ITV dating show, *Take Me Out*. You'll hear a truly amazing range of female accents. It's a programme that ought to give the word 'diversity' a good name.

A good question to put to the girls, without being patronising, would be to ask, 'What is a London accent?' (Answer: Estuary English, because it's mainly spoken around and near the River Thames and its estuary.) If you speak Estuary English, you will mix Standard English or RP, with some cockney features thrown in. On a show like *Take Me Out*, there's a fair chance that some contestants would say, '*Es-stew-ary*, what's an es-stew-ary?' 'Come dahn London mate, and I'll show yer!'

Somewhat incredibly, another male comedian, Peter Kay, was born, like Paddy Guinness, in the same town in Greater Manchester, in Farnworth, Lancashire. Paddy McGuinness has a unique way of talking about 'ORSES. He was briefly interviewed at Aintree's Grand National meeting (2016) and seemed chuffed (chŭffed) to be asked for his opinion. '*For sum-one laak meself 'oo duzn't gnaw m⊠ch abaa' 'ORSE racin'…* 'Still, that's all part of his charm.

(Should you want to watch all gender, full-on swearing on TV and be in 'chav-and-cheap' heaven, simply tune in to one of the biggest freak shows on earth, *Celebrity Big Brother Live Eviction*. They call it the 'CBB House' but, *to be honest*, it's more like a zoo for rabidly dysfunctional misfits. For innocuous silliness try watching ITV's *Pick Me!* The contestants appear to be on day release from 'loony bins'. Players are told they can 'go from zero to hero' by getting a question right. If you want to really go for it and get 'spaced out' by moronic incredulity, try Keith Lemon's *Celebrity Juice* on ITV2.)

Whilst on the subject of 'tuning in' to TV shows, BBC One's *Strictly Come Dancing* presenter, Tess Daly, invites viewers at the end of the show to 'TOON in next week', which has the opposite effect on me. She's married to Vernon Kay, which I suppose in pronunciation terms is like 'two peas in a pod'.

## Crafting on TV

What follows is probably not really within the ambit of relevant topics but I just wanted to mention some of the teleshopping shows on Freeview. Take createandcraft.tv. I am not in any way criticising either content or delivery or those who like 'crafting'. Being creative is really important in helping everyone to lead a fulfilling life. I just sometimes wonder how much 'brain power' is expended on 'craft creations' when it might be put to better use. Of course, adults now have their own colouring books to help them relax and what they do in their spare time is entirely their own business.

Perhaps the gripe is just with the sleek selling terminology that makes such things attractive. For example, you can have a 'gate-fold cut, themed on florals and flourishes'; you can add your own 'sentiments' to 'concept cards', make little boxes with a butterfly on top of a pentagon box cut-out, all 'super super simple, super easy', especially when you've got 'flexi-pay options'. You can start making 'Gift of Christmas' creations from mid-August, *Just look at the detailing on that!* Stick a 'sentiment' on too. In fact, after cursory glancing at what's on offer, most of the images for crafting are horribly 'twee', sickly sentimental and even childish; they seem fine for eight or nine year olds but not really for grown-ups except those confined to care homes and nursing homes with little scope to do anything.

You hear all the usual sales ploys: 'I wouldn't even think about it. I'd just grab it.' Or, 'At this price we're giving 'em away.' Pointing to a cut-out stamp (or was it a die?), the eager presenter says, 'You've got your horn of plenty, *or* your fruit *băss-kit*' (rhymes with lass-). No mention here of cornucopias.

You attach 'heartfelt creations' with 'regal borders', along 'magnolia lane(s)' with tassels added; you've got 'your butterfly coming off your trellis' and there are many 'festive flourishes', pop-up template dies, 'enchanted escapes' with a frayed lace look etc. that can be embossed and/or cut from 250gsm card stock. The male presenter of one set of 12 zodiac signs got so enthusiastic about them that he said, 'Here's your *stardiac*, I mean zodiac' when he meant signs of the zodiac. But lots of brain power is also expended on hobbies like crosswords, Sudoku, puzzle books, word games, flowers-by-number starter kits, noting down train or aircraft numbers, building terrariums, fish tanks, model trains, making miniatures, jigsaw puzzles, carving walking sticks, so all crafters please accept an apology in advance.

You can get Sudoku for kids, Sudoku for fanatics, and web Sudoku with the frightening tagline: '***Billions*** of Free Sudoku Puzzles to Play Online[1]… from easy to evil with ***unlimited play!*** Isn't that a frightening thought – billions of Sudoku puzzles to be completed with unlimited play? How much time would literally be thrown away? (Literally is correct here, unlike the person who might say, after just losing out on an Olympic gold record, 'I was literally gutted.') It's not so far removed from Jeremy Irons' soothing voice-over for Sky movies: 'Over a thousand movies on Sky, all on demand.' Watch them all and be 'locked up' for more than 83 days (and nights)...

There's usually a proverb or maxim that serves everyone well. In this case, I think it should be 'Each to his own' or 'Each to their own.'

Or a Tommy Cooper joke. 'I said, "It's serious doctor, I've broken my arm in 20 places." He said, 'Well stop going to those places.'

# CHAPTER SIX

*More game and reality shows – Mrs May 'a big pointless pot of low-fat yoghurt' – Giles Coren to eat children 'if Jeremy Corbyn wins next election' – 'sticklers' à la David Starkey – dress rules for men – dialects – 'the fat, bald bloke on MasterChef' – some word meanings explained – David Dimbleby in Doncaster – long and short 'a's'*

G AME AND REALITY SHOWS have a lot to answer for (as well as the truly detestable *Big Brother* and *Celebrity Big Brother*). As soon as I hear (on that show) the word 'housemates' or an actual time such as, '4.28aayemm', I cringe. 'Be prepared for Ō-ffensive language.' No sooner have you got used to one show like *All Star Family Fortunes*, and have grown accustomed to Vernon Kay's brash style of presenting when along comes another new star or craze, like Bradley Walsh and the TV show *Cash Trapped*, 'based on one of Bradley's original ideas', with 'a genuinely unique twist'. It doesn't seem, however, to have gone down too well with viewers so far. Another new show is called *Go For It*. I was looking at a Marlborough bun in a shop recently when an assistant suggested the same.

It starts with 'a series of fast-paced question round(s)'. The one I briefly watched had a contestant called 'Dean', who seemed remarkably laid back. (Dean should be congratulated as he won the game and a very good prize.)

*Bradley Walsh:* 'What substance makes the Cliffs of Dover white? You know, the white cliffs of Dover?'

*Dean:* 'Pass.'

*Bradley Walsh:* 'What country in Britain does "Caledonia" refer to?'

*Dean:* 'Dunno.'

*Answers:* chalk; Scotland

For another cringing 'fun panel show' with little fun, you can't beat Channel 5's, *It's Not Me, It's You.* The jokes are banal (US pronunciation, b-ānal), crude, in poor taste. To get 'laffs', panel members expatiate on excretory and reproductive functions, clap themselves silly like performing monkeys, and keel over at their own sordid 'jokes'.

Sandi Toksvig (alma mater: Girton College, Cambridge) hosts one of the few game shows with some genuinely difficult questions, *Fifteen to One.* Some of the easiest questions are sometimes on *In It To Win It,* hosted by Dale Winton, of *Supermarket Sweep* fame, a bizarre game that, inter alia, involved piling up items into shopping trolleys. However 'tacky' some of these shows are, they could *never* be as scary as some US reality shows, like *The Real Housewives of Atlanta* (actually any other '*Real Housewives*' programme too). Being forced to watch this is almost enough to tip the balance into insanity. The over manicured, over coiffed and painted 'housewives', with their massively oversized American egos make my hormone levels rapidly recede to vanishing point, and the American male presenter (and guests) seem like craven wimps. On the subject of more-difficult-than-average quiz shows, *Only Connect* on BBC Two, chaired by Victoria Coren Mitchell (alma mater: St John's College, Oxford) is harder than most. No one watching the show probably ever thinks about the author of the injunction, 'Only connect!' (From the epigraph to E.M. Forster's 1910 novel, *Howards End*.)

## 'A big pointless pot of low-fat yoghurt'

There's a new show called *500 Questions*, chaired by Victoria's brother, Giles Coren (alma mater: Westminster School, Keble College, Oxford). Watching the first ever show, I noted that Giles thinks the way to pronounce 'Charlotte' is 'char-lot' (as in char lady) rather than *shar*-lot; he knows most of the 28 Muppets in the *Muppet Show* by heart; and like similar shows, there is the frightening line, emphasised for the sheer dread of it, 'Get this wrong, and **you will go home with nothing!**' (I am sure contestants must be able to claim expenses and an appearance fee, if only to compensate for the likelihood of being ribbed and joshed by Giles. One could hardly go home after appearing on *500 Questions* and own up to earning 'diddly-squat'. He's pretty good at this, having learnt how to slate and slag off some restaurants in his restaurant reviews.) However, in a huge headline in *The Times*[1], Giles Coren wrote, of PM Theresa May, 'May is a big pointless pot of low-fat yoghurt.' He describes her as 'twitchy' and 'humourless'. In response to bookmakers making Corbyn the 5/1 favourite to win the next election, Coren declares: 'If that happens I will eat both my children, raw, in front of the Cenotaph at dawn.' And Boris Johnson is nothing but a 'walking corpse'. Good luck if you elect to go on *500 Questions*. 'Which British prime minister has been described as "a big pointless pot of low-fat yoghurt"?' (I know this book has a few 'gripes' but not to the extent of describing a Tory PM as a pointless pot of yoghurt. Perhaps Giles thinks in terms of food/restaurant analogies. Here we have a pointless pot of sour cream, soaked in Bullingdon Club leftovers [George Osborne]; then, a giant vat of lard steeped in Keighley brine [Eric Pickles], and oh look, a delicate, diaphanous Scottish sushi [Nicola Sturgeon].)

In the paragraph above, note 'diddly-squat'; this is one of the favourite words of German stand-up comedian, Henning Wehn. How could a German pick this up? Perhaps by being such a great observer of the English and their way of life. He certainly tells lots of jokes about us – such as how we *like* to fight each other trying to get to the front of a kebab queue.

As an aside, Boris Johnson's speech at the Conservative Party Conference (2016) showed touches of brilliance and statesmanship – an improved performance. If this was a 'walking corpse', I wouldn't mind being similarly disposed.

His humorous side was evident too: 'The EU is trying to veto the ivory ban despite having a president called Donald Tusk.' He was careful to pronounce it as in an elephant's tusk rather than the correct 'tŭsk'.

Another game show on BBC1 is called *Think Tank*, hosted by Bill Turnbull. He said in the last show I cursorily watched, 'Now, *tankers*, we have an arithmetical question for you. How many pints are there in a gallon?' If you had got that 'think tank' question right, answering 8 pints, you would have won £200. (I think I'll join a think tank.)

(It's not just game and reality shows that are to blame. You can add nearly all soaps like *Eastenders* and *Coronation Street*. In the former, standard fare is rowing [as in not in a boat but having rows, rhymes with rouse], shouting, argumentative 'cuss-heads', supposedly role models, who set abysmal parenting examples. Scriptwriters delight in getting in absurd solecisms and words mistakenly used for the real thing [malapropisms], such as intentionally mangling any difficult-to-pronounce or vaguely unfamiliar words. *Note:* standard fare is Phil 'bustin' a guuh' [gut] to 'do someone over', because ''e's got the 'ump and Shirley's crackin' up' in the next room.)

After being underwhelmed by *Cash Trapped*, I switched over to see Jeremy Corbyn giving a speech about the declining services being offered by the NHS. Mr Corbyn, who has latterly staged something of a comeback as Leader of the Labour Party, was having what is sometimes described as 'an impassioned rant' about '*amba*-lan-ces' (ambulances), which sounded just like 'amber-lănces'. Perhaps one of his most endearing qualities is his 'zany' habit of photographing manhole covers. Drain and manhole covers have their devotees, mainly for the historical perspectives they provide.

Whilst having no avowed intent to pass ad hominem or personal comments on Mr Corbyn, whose 'friends' are said to include Hamas and Hezbollah, it occurred to me that, as someone who survived a personal relationship with former lover Diane Abbott MP (alma mater: Newnham College, Cambridge; tutored by the illustrious historian Simon Schama, alma mater: Christ's College, Cambridge), he must be made of stern stuff indeed as two Labour politicians rarely agree on the same thing (such as trains being full or nearly full) without a degree of disagreement. I'm not sure this is a very good argument, *to be honest*.

*Note:* The several mentions of Jeremy Corbyn might seem unfair but are here by chance, and as nothing compared to critics such as the Jewish Labour donor who compared Jeremy Corbyn's inner circle to Nazi stormtroopers over escalating infighting in the party.[2] On a much lesser note, former shadow chancellor Ed Balls in his autobiography *Speaking Out* compared Corbyn's leadership style to a 'hard left Utopian fantasy'. That's from someone whose favourite culinary treat is an overcooked Yorkshire pudding with jam on top.

Ed Balls, however (alma mater: Keble College, Oxford; Harvard University), can dance a mean samba, as *Strictly Come Dancing* showed.

A common error (*should I instead say 'variation'?*) of pronunciation is to say 'bŭrry' (rhymes with 'Chicks and ducks and geese better *scurry*/when I take you out in the *surrey*/… with the fringe on top', *Oklahoma* soundtrack) for bury (same as berry). Perhaps it just depends what part of the country you come or '*coom*' from. Aristocrats have scions, the middle classes children or kids, and the lower class (especially in the south of England) have nippers, as in, ''Ow's yer nipper?'

## Some right 'sticklers'

The constitutional historian and TV presenter David Starkey (alma mater: Fitzwilliam College, Cambridge) prefers to say 'par-*li-a*-ment-ary' and 'par-*li-a*-ment' rather than 'par-le-men-tary' and 'par-le-ment'. That's because he's something of a 'stickler' by character and nature, at least that's my opinion. Since the word 'Parliament' comes from the French *parler* (talk, talking), it might seem slightly affected to insist on the 'lia' in the middle, in particular the 'i' (ee) sound between the 'l' and the 'a'. (I was gratified to hear the constitutional expert, crossbencher Lord Lisvane stick with the pronunciation 'par-le-ment', despite being a 'stickler' par excellence, I would imagine. Lord Lisvane (alma mater: Lincoln College, Oxford) should know quite a bit about languages as he read Old Norse, medieval Welsh and Anglo-Saxon there.) For those who might want to know more about Lord Lisvane, he is Robert James Rogers, Baron Lisvane KCB, DL, a notable Clerk of the

House of Commons (2011–14), who served for over four decades in the House.

Sticklers in my view like to say '*nego-see-ate*' for nego-shee-ate (negotiate) and the same goes for appreciate. No doubt both are acceptable with the latter just preferred (EmmaSayer is very clear on which she prefers. Try listening.[3]) Nicholas Soames is not that kind of stickler, I think. He would just wade in and *nego-shee-ate*, as a guess. However, according to Tom Utley of the *Daily Mail*, Lord Soames likes to sport *five* buttons on the sleeves of his jacket, which is a bit like over-stickling.[4] The cardinal dress rule for men's jackets (unless *very* casual) is no less than four and no more than four buttons. Sport three buttons and you've been shopping downmarket, certainly not in Jermyn Street. [Correction: Sir Nicholas, wearing a magnificent pair of maroon, knee-length socks was heard on *Newsnight* with Emily Maitlis saying 'iss-you' and not 'iss-shoe' (for issue), so perhaps he is a 'negot-*see*-ate' man after all. Heavy-jowled Lord Soames has a curious habit, when just about to answer or having answered a question, of rolling his tongue quickly from one side of his mouth to the other, a bit like a bulldog getting ready to make a stand. He wouldn't stand for *the cloomsy doock*, one suspects. He'd give it a good kicking, all the way back to St James' Park.]

My guess too, but it's only a guess, is that David Starkey CBE, FSA, a Visiting Professor of the University of Kent, will also be a 'stickler' when it comes to pronouncing the word '*en*velope'. The verb 'to envelop' has just the one way to pronounce but the noun 'envelope' originally came from the French, and educated classes liked to show their learning by mimicking the French, as in '*arrn*-vel-ope'. However, the word has been in use in English for several hundred years, and has been anglicised as a result. So, in my book, you can say '*en*velope' (rhymes with *en*gender or the *en* rule in printing, a dash larger than a hyphen but smaller than 'an em dash'). Insisting on '*arn*-velope' can be seen as affected, which would, in a manner of speaking, fit in with David Starkey's unique style, as is his use of the word 'substantial', which, rather than with a short 'a' to begin with sounds like 'sub-staan-shul', like the long final 'a' in Afghanistān. (Do you think using a phonetic alphabet might be easier?')

As he has been called 'the rudest man in Britain', a soubriquet bestowed on him by the *Daily Mail* for his *Question Time* appearances, has described the Catholic Church as 'corrupt and riddled with corruption from top to bottom',[5] and once declared that Scotland, Ireland and Wales are 'feeble little countries',[6] and likened Alex Salmond (at the time Scottish First Minister) to a 'Caledonian Hitler',[7] I feel confident he wouldn't mind these harmless and negligible little brickbats.

Whilst on the subject of Scotland, it seems one must never underestimate the power of dialects, of the vernacular. Robert (Robbie) Burns was a master. This, 'A Red, Red Rose' is from the 1794 original:

*As fair art thou, my bonie lass.*
*So deep in luve am I;*
*And I will love thee still, my Dear,*
*Till a' the seas gang dry.*

The only good thing to say about obituaries is that sometimes they throw up the sort of information you would never normally know about. Jamie Stuart's obituary in *The Times*[8] is one case in point. A former door-to-door salesman, actor and storyteller, he became a bestselling author by retelling the Gospel stories in Glasgow vernacular, so much so that one book, *The Gospel of Mark*, was reprinted more than 50 times!

Reading this has engendered some humility. What is it about 'ordinary speech' that is so engrossing? Stuart wrote (he died on July 2016, aged 95): 'The vernacular is powerful, pungent and totally accessible.' So what kinds of words and pronunciations did he use that people loved them so much?

Here are some brief examples from titles such as *A Scot's Gospel*, *Auld Testament Tales* and *Glasgow Gospel*:

*The Nativity:* 'Mary wis expectin her bairn an her time wis nearly due.'

*David and Goliath:* 'Weel, come oan then, ya big scrawny plook!'

*Parable of the Good Samaritan:* 'Right then, Jimmy, jist you dae the same.'

*The Prodigal Son:* 'It wasnae lang before he wasted his hale fortune oan the bevvy, an the parties, and livin' it up.'

To rephrase the reason or rationale for *The Pocket Book of (Proper) English Pronunciation*: one cannot criticise any regional accents, dialects or local vernaculars. They are rich is local tradition, history and culture. So, I suppose '*the groompy/cloomsy doock*' must be allowed to stand, damn it, as in, if that's the way you want to say it, pal, it's really none of anyone's business but your own. 'You like to-may-toes and I like to-mah-toes' – there's no argument (perhaps excepting the rest of this chapter, and one or two pages in between). Don't *let's call the whole thing off*, just yet!

So then we are stuck with affected pronunciations, like 'scōne' and 'cawst' and errors such as 'ath-a-lete', affidavids, and decrepid assessories, probly (see p. 104). That leaves something to work on, *dunnit*. Sorry, I mean, doesn't it?

Time to end that section too but not before a few more 'plain tales from the hills'. The TV *MasterChef* man, Gregg Wallace, would put me off eating any food if I had to listen to him for too long (ditto John Torode). Mr Wallace is great with phrases like, 'Dee-lightful. I'm in chocolate 'eaven.' You wouldn't think so, I guess, but he happens to be quite humble in some ways, unlike the blustering and overbearing personality he can show on MasterChef. He has described himself as 'just the fat, bald bloke on MasterChef who likes pudding'.[9] He once traded as a costermonger. That's one of those words that I thought I knew but didn't. I imagined it had something to do with fish for sale on a barrow but no, it describes a person who sells 'goods, especially fruit and vegetables, from a handcart in the street'. They were generally very competitive and used a 'loud sing-song cry or chant to attract attention'. Perhaps his no nonsense blustering style on *MasterChef* is understandable. On the plus side, his *Inside the Factory* programmes on BBC are genuinely worth watching. Naturally, as soon as you get one good programme, another *programmus horibilis* follows fast behind, like *Eat Well for Less*, with Gregg Wallace and Chris Bavin. Like shady characters they hide along super-market aisles, observing hapless shoppers 'trolley-piling' red traffic light pies, and bags of frozen chips a lesser person might use for weight training.

Returning to the long 'e's in some words, one gets, if perhaps one were a costermonger (note: coster*mung*er pronunciation, not '-monga'), 'a dee-vorce' (going on the dee-fensive now). But no, properly it's a *di*vorce (like the *di-* in divot). You go to a děbate and not a dee-bate (as Clive Myrie (and many others) says on BBC News); one is '*de*fensive' (rhymes with Guy *de* Maupassant). Unfortunately, if you haven't learnt to speak French by now, it's of little help.

## Some word meanings explained

If you should pass a Café Rouge, and spot the 'prix fixe' sign chalked on a board outside, without some knowledge of French, how would you know it was not '*pricks fix*' rather than *pree feex*?

Does longevity have a soft or hard 'g'?
How do you pronounce 'victuals'?
*What is a 'victual'?*
How do you say 'Prosciutto?'
And Açai? Quinoa? Crudités, brioche?

*Answers:*

- Longevity is pronounced with a hard 'g'. Like the 'g' in *grease* or *goat* and not the 'g' sound in the words 'The *gerbil* in the *gym*'
- Victuals is pronounced as 'vittals', like 'vitals' but with a short 'i'. A victual (vital) is food or provisions. The verb is 'to victual'
- Prosciutto (Italian, thinly sliced, dry cured ham) is pronounced 'pro-shoot-tow'
- Açai is 'ah-sigh-ee' (small, purple edible berry)
- Quinoa is 'keen-wah' (grain crop with very nutritious edible seeds)
- Crudités is 'krew-dee-tay' (mixed raw vegetables, usually with sauce dips)
- Brioche is 'bree-osh' (French, pastry with egg and butter, making it like enriched bread).

Pronunciation dictionaries were on sale in Victorian times, especially books explaining the intricacies of classical mythology – how to sound as if you knew what you were talking about when discussing caryatids and propylaea in Athens, notably the one forming the entrance to the Acropolis.

When Grand Tours (which could last from several months to several years) went out of fashion, along with any enthusiasm for things Neoclassical, the mythology and classical pronunciation dictionaries became curios for arcane collectors. Things became much more mundane as a result, *init*? The last word is but tongue-in-cheek, *naturellement*.

## Jeremy Paxman, and Dimbleby in Doncaster

Game shows from which someone might actually learn something useful would have to include *Mastermind* and the unique *University Challenge*. The latter is so helpful to get a glimpse of undergraduate 'eggheads' (a horrible word), reveal one's own intellectual shortcomings, and be guided in pronunciation, professorially, by Jeremy Paxman, who succeeded that other guru of the species, Bamber Gascoigne.

Paxman (alma mater: Malvern College, St Catherine's College, Cambridge) speaks English as an Englishman should; he gets few things wrong and doesn't need a BBC pronunciation unit behind him. I suppose you could include David Dimbleby, a former member of Oxford University's Bullingdon Club, best known for the BBC's *Question Time*, as another guide to good pronunciation (alma mater: Charterhouse, Christ Church, Oxford). Oddly, on Wikipedia, Dimbleby has no reference to his 'alma mater'; there is just an entry under 'Education'. I have my doubts (very minimal) about Dimbleby, because when I was watching a *Question Time* broadcast, he said, 'So, it's goodbye from Don-căster' (short 'a'), which admittedly would have been appropriate as *he was* in Don-căster, but I bet when he got home to his wife, if she had said, 'Where have you been, David?' his reply would have been 'Doncaster'. Not '-caster' as in căster sugar either, just Doncaster (almost like *Doncusta*). Then, there's the small matter of the six-legged scorpion tattooed on his right shoulder at the age of 75. He said it was 'a dream come true'. Cue cliché: there's no accounting for tastes.

I believe Edgbaston is in Birmingham. I was relieved recently to hear some presenters refer to it as *Edge-ba-ston*, not the pronunciation that sounds like an assailant is hurling something at you, *Edge-BAST-on*. If you have noticed that there is no 'a' in the list of letters, as in Chapter Two, it's probably because I just, *to be honest*, 'don't want to go there'. Much of the divisions in British society are caused, I am sure, by vowels, and particularly the 'a' vowel. 'Where are you?' is a simple enough question, but the answer may not be.

> *Question:* Where are you?
> *Answer:* In the BATH
> (the 'a' rhymes, slightly, with bat)
> *Question:* Where are you?
> *Answer:* In the BARTH
> (rhymes with hearth or garth)
> Try saying, 'I'm having a *baarth* near the *hearth*' or

'I'm having a *băth* near the *hearth*.'
My *berth* is in the *baarth* near the *hearth* or
My *berth* (could be *bear-th*) is in the *băth* near the
*hearth*'.

Constituents (or constit-u-ents) of the entire country could only agree on the pronunciation of one word, *hearth*, from the words in italic.

Of course, I could be wrong, but does that suggest the 'hearth' is so integral to all of us, as the main feature or long-lost focus of our homes, that it sounds the same wherever you come from? Home is where the heart is? Heart and hearth have a lot in common.

## Some long and short 'a's

I suppose any compiler of errant pronunciations is up against it. You just can't change things or criticise. Some people like to say 'The green green gr*ass* of home', with the gr*āss* sounding the same (without the *gr-*) as Americans say 'ass'. Some people love to imagine falling onto a soft green carpet of gr-*ass*, perhaps wet with morning dew, in springtime, even in their own back yard or garden. Others fall on the gr-*arse*, and say to themselves, 'Oh green gr-*arse*! Oh green green gr-*arse* of home!'

It's a shame that words can cause divisions by being 'class identifiers', I mean how they are said. 'A rose by any other name would smell as sweet', said Shakespeare. But a rose is a rose in most parts of the country (the same in Lancaster as in York); you might get a Scottish bur with the 'r',

and some say 'rose' to rhyme with 'hose' and others 'rose'
to rhyme with 'wraws' or 'craws'. But grass, something as
simple as grass! Go back to the French Revolution and
you might be guillotined for saying 'gr-arse' and spared for
saying 'gr-ass'.

Is this 'the half (rhymes with barf) of it?' NO! It's not
the 'hăff' (rhymes with chaff or 'laff') of it either. Half (plural halves) is clearly an important little word. There must
be lots of things in the world capable of being divided by
two. Here are some:

- half a crown, half a dozen
- half-and-half
- halfback
- half-baked
- half binding
- half board
- half-cooked
- half-century
- half-cocked
- half-hearted
- half hitch
- half holiday (or 'oliday – if Fleet Street editor,
    Kevin Maguire)
- half-inch
- half-life
- half-light
- half mast

- half measure
- half moon
- halfpenny (also ha'penny)
- half price
- half-sister
- half-term
- half-time
- half-truth
- halfway
- halfwit

With pronunciation of the above, it's mainly binary too. It's the long or the short 'a' again.

# CHAPTER SEVEN

*Difficult words to pronounce – some explanations – apocryphal story from Sir Nicholas Soames, grandson of Winston Churchill – 'slips of the tongue' in Parliament – gerrymander or gerrymonger*

WHAT ARE THE MOST difficult words to pronounce? *Note*: the theme is not to compile a long list of difficult-to-say words; it's to point out that even simple ones can make people sound *stoo-pid* (or *stew-pid*) – with an odd proviso, they may sound perfectly right to whoever says them (and their peers) but not to others, or 't'others' as they say in the north.

*What do you fink?* As soon as someone says, 'I fink...' the chances are the speaker is incapable of much in the way of thinking. Radio 1 used to be a haven for illiterates. Perhaps it is now marginally better. Those who insist on saying 'aks' (arks) for 'ask' are just digging deeper into the hole. 'I fink I arksed 'im ou' like bu', *to be honest*, I don' ree-member any-ting.' Probably it would be a double negative – as in not remembering 'nuh-ting' or 'It doesn't taste no different than when I do my own cooking.' Shame on the teachers who can't be bothered to make a difference. Shame on them all! Hundreds of hopeless 'teachers' who should be inspiring their classes with a love of language, the English language, yet who seem to pass on nothing that would be of any use outside the classroom.

affadavid or affidavit
apocrapha, apocrypha or apocryphal
artbitry or arbitrary
assessory or accessory
decrepid or decrepit
dubya or double U
Eistetffod or Eisteddfod
expresso or espresso
fedral or federal
fort or forte (fortay)
Klu Klux Khan or Ku Klux Klan
minature or miniature
miniscule or minuscule
nucular or nuclear
ordinance or ordnance
perogative or prerogative
probly or probably
prostrate or prostate
reoccur or recur
steatopigyeous or steatopygous
triathalon or triathlon, *also* decathalon or decathlon
Green witch or Greenwich (Gren-itch)
yeller card or yellow card

It seems as if there are several kinds of mispronunciation. It's not just the long or difficult words you find in medicine (e.g. *hyperprolactinaemia*, *hypertriglyceridaemia*, *atlantoaxial subluxation*); it's the ordinary everyday words that are mixed up with others that sound much the same or words that are misspelt and therefore mispronounced.

## Notes on some of the above

- The word 'affidavit' has its roots in the Latin *affidare*, which means 'to pledge'. It is a written, sworn statement of fact, voluntarily given, made under oath or on affirmation before a magistrate, judge or other officer of the court (and 'David' has nothing to do with it).

- The word 'apocrapha' is a misspelling of Apocrypha. The Apocrypha is the name given to a group of 14 biblical books of dubious authenticity, and usually unknown authorship, including 'gospels' not accepted as part of any particular 'canon', not considered as pukka 'Scripture'.

- Apocryphal is a rather good adjective (like avuncular), once popular with RP speakers, used to describe a somewhat doubtful statement or story, often put about as true (*see also* p. 119–20). A delightful apocryphal story comes from the portly Lord Soames, grandson of Winston Churchill.[1] It is worth repeating here.

Grandson Soames, when he was about five years old, had no idea how famous his grandfather was until someone told him. So, Soames found his way into the old man's bedroom, sneaking past valets, secretaries and other flunkies, and found him propped up in bed. There is no way of knowing if he had a cigar in one hand and a 'brandy snifter' in the other.

Coming straight to the point, he asked: 'Is it true, Grandpapa, that you are the greatest man in the world?'

'Yes, I am,' said Churchill. 'Now bugger off.'

- The Eisteddfod is an annual Welsh festival (pl. eisteff-fodau) with competitions for poetry and prose prizes. It has a quasi-druidic history, and all participants have to speak Welsh. This rule was waived when Princess Elizabeth was made a druidic bard princess in 1947 at an Eisteddfod ceremony, six years before she became queen.

- It's easy and convenient to ask for an '*ex*presso', but it won't make the coffee appear any faster. It's an espresso. The original Italian name was *caffè espresso* ('pressed-out coffee). [I don't know why the accent is not acute but grave other than it may have been the way it was written c. 150 years ago.]

- Nu-cu-lar or NUKE-yuh-luhr is a surprisingly common error. US presidents Jimmy Carter and George W. (hence Dubya) Bush used it. It's not hard to say 'nu-clee-ar' (NYOO-klee-uhr).

- An 'ordinance' is a county or municipal law; ordnance (as in Ordnance Survey – originally a military map or a map created for military use. 'Ordnance' means

mounted guns/artillery or a government branch deal-
ing with military stores, equipment and materials.)
Only yesterday I heard a news presenter say, 'The
Turkish army has moved up military ordinance in the
form of tanks and artillery towards the Syrian border.'
Having just been writing the above, I thought I've
got to re-check the definition of 'ordinance'. *Hey-ho!*
Guess what I found:

The noun 'ordinance':

1) an authoritative order
2) a religious rite
3) an archaic term for 'ordonnance' (which is
   a statutory instrument).

So much for the Turkish army, thanks to this news
presenter. [Weird and wonderful are the things you
can hear on news channels. After an earthquake in
Italy, the Pope broadcast a message on TV announcing the imminent, perhaps ongoing, *intercession* of
the Virgin to heal those affected by the quake. 'The
Virgin is embracing you with her motherly love.' My
first thought was can a virgin also be a mother; but
of course, this was *the* Virgin Mary, who conceived
things in her own way, with the help of God.]

• One prostrates oneself before an idol or a god in an
  act of submission. To lie prostrate means being face
  downward on the floor. The prostate gland in older
  men causes a lot of problems although when young the

prostate gland provides some useful extras to facilitate things sexual. If in doubt, please consult your doctor.

- Reoccur refers to things that happen every now and again (such as volcanic eruptions). You might have to wait 50 years for the same volcano to erupt again, but when it does, it's a reoccurrence. To recur means to happen (again) habitually, such as the sun rising every day or tides recurring twice a day.

- Someone with steatopygia, hence the adjective steatopygous, is a person with abnormal amounts of fat on the buttocks, a peculiarity of some races. The steatopygia, literally fat, suet or tallow on the buttocks can be so pronounced (as in noticeable or conspicuous) as to allow a dinner tray to be placed there quite comfortably without falling off. It's pronounced not as steato*pyg*ia (as in *pig*eon) but steatopygia as in pork *pie*s.

I'm sure you can work the others out for yourselves. The words on the right of the column above on p. 104 are correct, except for entries under 'ordinance' and 'prostrate', which could be either.

Some other difficult-to-pronounce words (especially for non-natives) include anemone, choir, colonel (rhymes with kernel), isthmus, sixth, plus of course most words of four or more syllables. Pronouncing 'squirrel' is also said to be hard for German speakers. You might ask why is there a 'p' in psoriasis, pronounced 'sore-rye-asis'. The Greek *psoriasis* means 'being itchy', from *psora* 'itch' and *psen* 'to rub'. So that explains it. According to Henning Wehn (see p. 88), you've probably got psoriasis because you've been 'itching to get to the kebab shop of a Saturday night'.

It's not that most words for Brits are hard to pronounce for the reasonably or even the marginally fluent. It's more that ordinary words get the wrong treatment, as in, 'You, didn't know that, didya?' or 'Bai-sick-ly (as if commenting from the saddle of a bicycle), in a nu'shelw, Oiy was laaike, oh my god, Oive dun it!'

## Occasional 'slips of the tongue'

One might mention MPs' occasional 'slips of the tongue' too, since they seem to crop up in this pocket book with some regularity. The well-liked conservative MP Peter Bone, when talking on issues of health (it is said he sometimes likes to mention his wife, Mrs Bone), came up with 'multiple scer-losis' (instead of sclerosis) and shadow treasury minister Peter Dowd said that it had all been a 'duh-băck-el' (debacle) (please see EmmaSaying for her opinion).

Occasionally, the really sharp wordsmith can hear new words on TV or the radio – mangled pronunciations or completely new ones. For example, the word 'gerrymandering' (gaining a political advantage by redrawing boundaries) may mistakenly become *gerrymongering*.[2] The origin or etymology of 'gerrymander' would make a good question for quiz shows where the questions are too easy. *To be honest*, I didn't know the meaning of the word either, except that it had something to do with politics. If you don't know, the answer is below.

It helps to have friends who may know words you don't. For example, after I had teased one old friend for saying piano (pee-ann-no) like 'pee-ahn-no', which is perhaps the way Sir Peregrine Worsthorne might say it, he caught me out by informing me that the Hungarian conductor Georg Solti was not, as I thought 'Salty' but 'Sholl-tee; and the Jewish word chutzpah (meaning self-confidence or audacity) is pronounced as 'hutspah' or 'hudspah' with the 'huts-' part to rhyme with 'mutts' (as pronounced in the north) and the 'spah' just like a spa. No sound of a 'ch' anywhere!

Other words that may confuse non-native speakers would fill a pocket dictionary. What about 'bough' and 'cough' and 'rough'? Could cause a hiccup or is it a hiccough? Or 'dough' and 'tough'? 'Stop kowtowing to that man and give me a tow. No, not a toe, a tow!" Or a puce lettuce (an unusual variety), or even 'here' and 'there'? Would you tip the refuse man or refuse him alms with folded arms? For 'have a go fun', *see* Appendix 1.

The verb to gerrymander is a portmanteau of two words, the name of a US state governor with the surname 'Gerry' and the amphibious, lizard-like creature known as a *salamander*. When boundaries in Massachusetts were redrawn by Democrats in 1812, that party was handed a distinct electoral advantage. A cartoon appeared at the same time satirizing the new shape of the district's boundaries. The district in question was drawn to look like a bizarre dragon-like monster, likened to the shape of a salamander.

# CHAPTER EIGHT

*Often or 'offen' – 'them' and 'those' – 'again' and 'agen' –
rolling your 'r's – crafting and quilting – maxed out
on toadstool fairies and 'amstas*

'**D**O YOU COME HERE often?' may seem an innocuous enough question but within it lurks the
dangerous conundrum of the lurking 't'. Whether one
should say 'off-en' or 'off-ten' was once the subject of a
long-winded BBC RP pronunciation guide in the previous century. The consensus today is no 't' please. Other
't's' have dropped out, such as the 't' in 'soften' (soff-en).
Similarly, with words like 'handkerchief' and 'handsome',
which have long dispensed with the 'd', though it remains
in the spelling. The last time I heard George Osborne pronouncing it, however, it was of*t*en, with a 't'!

Fowler, in his *Modern English Usage*, came up with a
remarkable if acerbic verdict. The pronunciation of the 't'
in 'often' was 'practised by two oddly consorted classes –
the academic speakers who affect a more precise enunciation
than their neighbours...and the uneasy half-literates who
like to prove they can spell'. Hyacinth Bucket of *Keeping*

*Up Appearances* likes to talk of 'man-new-ver-ing' (like 'hewvering', as in hoovering) rather than 'man-noo-ver-ing' (manoeuvring), an affected, if not academic, enunciation in her case.

It's surprising how many people say they 'can't be doing' (with something or other).

'Brexit? Nah, can't be doing with it.'

'Stay in the EU? Nah, can't be doing with that, neither.'

But when it comes to 'them' and 'those', they should 'be doing with it'.

## Them and those

My daughter's onetime boyfriend didn't make too good an impression as he walked behind her going up the stairs. I think he was talking about old broadsheet newspapers. He said, 'I suppose people got used to great big newspapers – in them days.' Downstairs, in the kitchen, I froze. Or rather, I was transfixed to the spot in the hearing of 'in **them** days', as if someone had just swatted me, like a fly, with a big fat newspaper.

He was, to be fair, a very pleasant young man. (Note here the use of 'pleasant' to describe a person. It carries no undertones. The English are great on *undertones*, which is similar to 'damning with faint praise'. For instance, if I had said he was '*plausible*', the word often carries [disguised] pejorative meaning.)

After 'a quiet word' later, she accepted my obser-vation, and agreed that she, too, had a dislike of being within earshot of someone who spoke of 'them' rather than 'those'. This is not unfair criticism, in an age when one must be as fair to a bisexual transgender 'queer' as to a lusty heterosexual – but one must look to the context. It might not have been acceptable for the suitor of my daughter to chat about what happened '*in them days*' but if I heard the same from an old stalwart of a local, even a 'yokel' (an unfair name from a townsperson to describe country folk), someone somewhere deep in the countryside propping up a pub bar, I would be honoured. Shakespeare loved plain-speaking ruffians be they Sir John Falstaff or his friends (knaves) like Bardolph with his bright red nose or the swaggering Pistol.

Looking through some old notes, I found a letter sent to *The Times* and to my surprise found it published there (15 October 1999). It was an ongoing discussion about whether school exams were getting easier. I had written that '…you need only look at what is being taught. In my ten-year-old daughter's Key Stage Two English book was this:

> Let's get this straight – if you get 'them' and 'those' muddled in the test, you will be losing marks. Lots of people use these words differently, but when you're marked, this is the way to do it… Them is a dead cool word – it's a pronoun…it saves you having to repeat the word again. It's not about whether you 'speak proper', it's just about

how you write them in the test so you don't lose marks. It boils down to this – don't write 'them books' or 'them earwigs' or whatever.

Clearly I had been biased from the start.

## Again and again

When is a gain not a gain? When it's again (pronounced a-gen) to rhyme with a pen. From this you could fairly conclude being a competent lexicographer is not my forte. The idea of contrasting 'a-gen' and 'a-gain' began confidently enough but I am not sure it would meet with a professor of logic's approval. *A-gain* can be used for more emphasis but 'a-gen' is preferable. About half a century ago (perhaps more) the BBC insisted on 'a-gen' as part of their rules of pronunciation for presenters.

*Hopefully*, I had switched on the TV to enjoy a quiet evening at home without having to worry much about what was on.

It was at that time wall-to-wall Olympics. To my astonishment (and frisson of pedantic horror) the first sentence I heard was: 'He's the only man to *ree-tain* (retain) an Olympic *decathalon*.' The BBC sports reporter continued with, 'It's *hish-tree* in the makin'. We knew he wanted some *ree-dress* (redress) for when he missed out last time.' As far as I know, if you re-dress, you get dressed again whereas 'rĕdress' means to remedy or set right.

# Rolling your 'r's

The next channel was a detective whodunit set in Scotland. Have you ever heard a Scot say 'murder'? The 'r's' roll mightily and frightfully and, *to be honest*, it sounds as if he's murdering the word too. It's all down to what linguists call 'the rhotic r'. That's when the 'r' after a vowel is 'rolled', as in, 'a rhotic speaker pronounces as a consonant postvocalic "r", the "r" after a vowel', as in 'world'. Non-rhotic speakers include RP speakers, who don't make any effort at all to sound the 'r'.' That's 'rhoticism' for you. To get an idea what the rhotic 'r' sounds like, just tune in to one of archaeologist Neil Oliver's TV programmes, like *Coast* or catch Nicola Sturgeon proposing a new referendum on independence for Scotland. When she says, 'Scotland's voice needs to be heard around the *worrrlld*,' the rolling 'r' sounds like it could travel from Holyrrrood to Inverrrness. (Holyrood is pronounced 'holly-rood' by the way. Usually the '-rood' is 'short', sounds like 'wood'.)

A note on those who can't pronounce even a silent 'r', as in 'The wemarkable wemnants of the Weign of Terror'. A notable authority or exerciser of this speech 'impediment' was the Liberal Democrat politician, Roy Jenkins, Baron Jenkins of Hillhead OM, PC. Suggestions as to the word or term for such a linguistic feature range from dysrhotic, hypolingual /r/, and the Winchester R (from Winchester College, where the current pupils are known as Wykehamists (wick-ham-ists), and whose parents pay over £36k per annum for their scions to board). A few have suggested 'a ranker', calling it 'iwwitating'.

## Crafting and quilting

Surely there was something on the crafting channel. Yes, there were shiny things called 'mirri mats' for when you 'mat and lay', and 'stamps' to make cards. You could choose a Halloween stamp, 'and if you want to distress it, put some cobwebs in, and you can mix and match them all!'

Choose a 'You're so special' sentiment for the fairy on the toadstool or a 'Wishing you a rainbow of happiness' sentiment. A small frog appears at the bottom of a stamp. 'Oh look, we've got a frog. Where did he come from?' There were also alphabets (including one written in distressed ink) you could cut out, emboss, stick or stamp on cards with names of your friends. 'There are so many names out there now, so it's great to have the option of personalising.'

After that there was 'quiltin'. 'Bēfore (B4) jettin' off sumwhere ohh' (hot), there's loads of things that comes [*sic*] with it (a machine for cutting triangle shapes to make quilts). The programme featured an American lady who travelled the world, demonstrating the cutting power of the machine. Her name was 'Anty (as in 'ant') (Auntie) Jean. She described herself as *'an innernational educator'*. Only an American could say, 'It's a real traditional plastic pattern.' This is not to decry the creative range and skills of traditional quilters in the UK, some of whom form groups that have lasted for decades, hold workshops, and make beautiful things. (*Did you know* how much work goes into hand-made quilts? A 'proper' quilt can take about £150–£200 worth of fabric, and if made by hand about 200 hours of quilting! Yet the prices quoted by some quilters are so very modest. If you are in need of one for a double or single bed, try www.rosemaryrabbitquilts.co.uk.)

'This is a little bit *in*promptu', said one announcer, 'so it's a nice little DYEversion.' After consulting EmmaSaying (emmasaying.com), it seems you can say diversion with a long or short 'i' but inpromptu? No, it's most definitely *im*promptu.

At last I tuned in to *Coronation Street* (by accident, let's be honest about it). I heard a young man say, '*Tek care o' pets? 'E coud'na e'en look afta an AMSTA*', the first time in my life I have ever heard the friendly rodent referred to as an 'amsta.

Not long after I was fast asleep. I had 'maxed out' on mispronunciations, toadstool fairies, and 'amstas.

# CHAPTER NINE

*Times Diary (TMS) – apocryphal story about philosopher Bertrand Russell – three more tips (three words to make sure you say correctly) – accents in the UK – cod have 'regional accents' – female grime rappers – words in families – the importance of speech in human evolution*

ONE OF THE BEST ways to puncture 'pronunciation pomposity' is to refer to one of those 'apocryphal stories', sometimes quite unconnected, as a kind of humorous displacement activity. One simply forgets all about *ath-a-leets*, *scōnes*, and the *cawst* of jam tarts.

And (Hemingway is said to have begun the craze for beginning sentences with the preposition) reading the *Times Diary* (TMS) can sometimes throw up some tales that allow a rather pleasant wave of good humour to wash over all the absurdities. Here is one I found (*after* the one about the bike) not long ago (it *might* be true though, and not apocryphal), a very good tale about philosopher Bertrand Russell. His is a name I can never easily forget as my father once looked up from a book he was reading, and said to me, 'Did you know that Bertrand Russell, who enjoyed cycling along country lanes, once came off his bicycle and fell into a ditch? When he picked himself up, *at that very moment*, he decided he was no longer in love with his wife.'

I could not see any reasonable connection between coming off his bike and deciding he wasn't in love with his wife, other than that the mind of a great philosopher is likely to be unlike the minds of the rest of us.

Quoting from the *Times Diary* (the possibly apocryphal story comes from the distinguished philosopher and academic A.C. Grayling, master of the independent New College of Humanities (founded by him).[1] When speaking at the Edinburgh book festival, discussing how his view of education had been shaped by Bertrand Russell, '...he recalled Russell's experimental Beacon Hill School and said that when a bishop visited he was shocked to have the door opened by a naked boy. "Good God," said the bishop, to which the free-thinking lad nonchalantly replied, "There isn't one."'

## Three more tips to get right

A friend of mine whose father flew Spitfires in the Second World War (with the rank of wing commander) said there were three words you could always rely on to reveal the level of someone's education and background. He probably said this at least twenty years ago but it's still valid. Say these and you'll give the game away. Of course, there are other verbal faux pas, such as saying 'execitive' for executive and even something as innocuous as this sentence. *Girl to boyfriend in supermarket*: 'Why didn't you buy the bu'er as wahl?' Of course, 'bu'er' with a 'glottal stop' is not the best way to say butter, and 'as wahl' (rhymes with David Walliams) is a funny way of saying 'as well' but surprisingly common. Last night a weatherman spoke of 'clouds in corn wall' (as in a wall of corn) when really I think it's 'Cornwŭl'.

The three words are in this sentence: *The new Foreign Secretary did not recognise the new state, with its dubious claims to power, prestige and regal pomp, et cetera.*

I wonder if you can see them without glancing further down the page. There's just time for this aside, before you find out. The same friend travelled to Winchester and back by train last summer on Southern Rail, which on a normal weekday runs about 2240 services.

Frustrated by delay caused by a 'strike' (reduced services) that day, and I suppose to amuse himself because there was little to do stuck on a railway platform, and knowing about my interest in 'locutions', he sent me this text.

*Spokesman for southern rail: 'Our strike 'as been backed up by safety concerns issued by the reggerlay'er.'*

This time it's all about the 'u' and disappearing 't' in 'regulator'!

'The new Foreign *Secetery* did not *reconise* the new state, with its dubious claims to power, prestige and regal pomp, *eckcetra*.

- secretary
- recognise
- et cetera (etc.)

Instead of sec-re-tree, the word is often said as 'sec-e-terry' or se-ca-tree.

Instead of re-cog-nise, it becomes 'rec-con-ise', without the 'g'.

Instead of et cetera, it's mispronounced as eckcetera, egg-cetra, etc.

By the way, the Foreign Secretary has the use of Chevening House in Sevenoaks, Kent. The official residence of the Foreign Secretary has 115 rooms set in 3500 acres. In 2016, Theresa May declared that Foreign Secretary Boris Johnson must share the building with fellow ministers David Davis and Liam Fox. This led to a conference jibe from Jeremy Corbyn: 'Theresa May and her three-legged team of fractious Brexiteers squabbling about who goes to the Chevening country estate at weekends.' The Prime Minister's country house retreat, set in more than 1000 acres, is Chequers, or Chequers Court in Buckinghamshire.

## Accents in the UK

Did you know there are at least 56 accents in the UK? A YouGov poll in 2015 found that the least attractive in the British Isles was the Brummie accent. Top of the list was the Southern Irish accent, followed by Received Pronunciation with the Welsh in third place.

For a hearty 'Teeside brogue', you can do no better than to watch and listen to Steph McGovern on *BBC Breakfast*. In a *Daily Express* interview, she said: 'I think people tend to underestimate you when you have a Northern accent, for instance when you have to talk to the CEO of an international company…But then when I'm talking to someone in a factory, it's just like being with my mum's mates.' One viewer was so put out by her accent that he offered to send her £20 towards 'correction-therapy', to improve her 'terrible Northern accent'. Put her in an interview with Paddy McGuinness and Vernon Kay, and he'd probably up his offer to £40 or even £60.

I watched *BBC Breakfast* for five minutes when Steph was presenting. Could I spot any anomalies? Two leapt off the screen, instead of the page in seconds. Obama's wife was 'Mee-*chell*' rather than 'Mee-*shell* (Michelle) and she liked her 'karry-ŏcki' style (rhymes with hockey). (I'm sure there's an 'oak' in karaoke.)

## Cornish and Geordie cod mix-up

It's hard to forget that catchy little tune from the north with its strong Geordie accent, 'When the Boat Comes In' (or 'Dance Ti Thy Daddy'). I think it was a fishing boat coming in. It was reported (October 2016) by Professor Steve Simpson from the University of Exeter that cod 'speak' (via their swimbladders in thumps and growls with different frequencies) in 'regional accents'. Cornish cod migrating north looking for colder waters may find it difficult to understand Scouse cod (and vice versa) and have difficulty ATTRACTING mates – 'can't follow the lingo, like'.

## More on accents

The South (Sarf) London accent is well known if not exactly attractive. To get an idea of what it's like, try listening to this YouTube clip. It sums it up pretty well in just a few minutes.[2]

A new accent infiltrating some London boroughs is 'Jafaican', a kind of multicultural hybrid, with mainly Jamaican input with some additions from West Africa and India/Bangladesh. It's becoming a distinctive patois in inner London and other cities, 'taking over' or even wiping out inner-city English accents. A word like 'face' may sound like 'fehs' in this 'fake Jamaican', which is where the name comes from. Cockneys would pronounce it more like 'fice' (as in vice).

Some Londoners who are black have also developed a very distinct accent, especially when they say a word such as 'like' or 'so' or 'with', so much so that with practice, it's possible to tell someone is black when you hear (but don't see them) speaking, such as with a voice-over on TV. There is also the infamous 'arks' or 'arx' for ask.

To get an idea of how society and language are changing, just watch these female MC 'grime rappers'.[3] One interviewed on BBC said 'Social media has been good for ar'ists (artists), d'yunowhaimean?'

# Words in families

Most families have bugbears or hobbyhorses when it comes to words. It's often the young laughing at the old or the old critiquing the young – not *criticising* – which is horrible. One word in our household is 'almond', of course instigated by none other than the author of this book! If I look at an almond tree, hold a shelled almond in my hand or eat an almond croissant, it is never an *ăl*-mond. It is an *aah*-mond. I disagree with 'EmmaSaying' on this. You can't argue for aah-mond by suggesting that no one would ask for smoked *săl*-mon (with a non-silent *'l'*) in a restaurant because word origins, roots, and styles of pronunciation (or accent) will always differ. Over time, pronunciations keep changing too.

Also, 'she' is plain wrong with 'almond'; I mean just listen here: https://m.youtube.com/#/watch?v=YTpZroijiI4. (I can't *beleeve* it! Morrisons has a new advert; 'When only the best will do'. A very smart female voice-over actually pronounces 'almond' as 'aah-mond'. And says 'Morrisons' rather than 'Morr-ee-sons'. What a turn-up!) The same voice-over lady suggests a Mawl-borough' wine when it should be 'Marl-borough' (though Malborrow-o in the US). Similarly, up to a point, it's Pall Mall, two short 'a's, and not 'The Mawl'. So, Pall Mall and The Mall have short 'a's' yet, weirdly at least in the UK, one talks of a 'shopping mawl' (morl).

The past tense of 'to eat' (ate) was usually pronounced as 'et', as in, 'Yesterday I ate (et) some salmon fishcakes' but now most people say 'ate'.

'Dad, is the car in the *garage*?' This is another word in the family that can evoke a parental cringe. Does it rhyme with mirage or marriage? It seems there are three possible pronunciations:

*We parked the car in the garage* (gă-raj) (rhymes with maha*raj*ah), equal stress on both syllables. Preferred, better class of gar-raj. ☺

*We parked the car in the garage* (rhymes with part*ridge*). Worst kind of 'garridge'! ☹

*We parked the car in the garage* (ga-RAJ), stress on second syllable. Upper class, affected. Okay if Bertie Wooster is instructing Jeeves.

Two popular phrases in our family are, 'Did you know' and 'Don't you know?'

I use the first, always very cautiously, so as not to appear too much of a pedant, as in, 'Do you know that schedule is pronounced *shed*ule and not *sked*ule?', or 'Do you know there are more than 56 accents in the UK?' or 'Do you know it's Coburn's Port and not Cockburn's?'

They have learnt to 'spar' quite well. When any one of the family tells me a fact, and it's obvious I don't know myself, they are very quick to respond archly, with, **'*Don't you know?*'**

One joke we can all share is, 'What do we own?' We were discussing the one-time extent of the British Empire and, scratching our heads to remember names, my daughter got out a large map, spread it on the table in front of us, and in a loud voice announced rather grandly, **'*Now, what*'**

***do we own?'*** There was silence, then huge laughter. I put it down to my daughter's confidence, gained I think from her all-girls independent school.

## The importance of speech in human evolution

Words are such wonderful things, as evinced by a new book. In *The Kingdom of Speech*, American writer Tom Wolfe[4] argues that speech is mankind's greatest artefact, the *sine qua non* of human development.

> *One bright night it dawned on me – not as a pro-found revelation, not as any sort of analysis at all, but as something so perfectly obvious I could hardly believe that no licensed savant had pointed it out before. There is a cardinal distinction between man and animal, a sheerly dividing line as abrupt and immovable as a cliff: namely, speech.*

Speech has given us the power to do anything – speech being '…the attribute of all attributes. Speech is 95%-plus of what lifts man above animal!'

'Speech was the first artefact, the first instance in which a creature – man – had removed elements from nature, in this case sounds, and turned them into something entirely new: strings of sounds that formed codes, codes called words…Speech not only ended the evolution of man, by making it no longer necessary for survival, but also the evolution of animals.

'In short, speech and only speech, has enabled us, we human beasts, to conquer every square inch of land in the world, subjugate any creature big enough to lay eyes on and eat up half the population of the sea.'

Powerful words (and their world-changing effects) have given us Jesus, Muhammad, Calvin, Marx, Freud, Darwin, Einstein et al. – along with Geoffrey Hughes as Onslow in *Keeping Up Appearances*: 'Bring us another beer, luv.' Joking aside, words have helped make the world.

# CHAPTER TEN

*Question tags – more on hypercorrection – the 'Home Counties' explained – a family history – Blackpool v the sunny south – Scottish independence and who owns all the grouse moors*

I HOPE YOU ARE ENJOYING this journey. It's been an 'amazing experience', hasn't it? The last two words, by the way, are known as a 'question tag', a figure of speech that seems to defeat many Englishmen and women. But, just for a moment, the journey: from 'Romford Man' in Essex to peers of the realm, to students of English, to country folk, whether in the dales, the valleys or the glens, the highland or lowlands, the Home Counties, 'and all'.

'He likes his cold grouse, isn't it?'

But we are not concerned here with question tags for students of English, *init?* One verb form must agree with the other (mustn't it?). (A note on the subject of hypercorrection [see p. 47]. Some foreign speakers know that 'isn't it?' is wrongly used sometimes [He always came to the church, isn't it?] and that 'init' is always wrong; the hypercorrection might take the form of 'wasn't it'; 'He always came to the church, wasn't it?' and it's still wrong. An eccentric example of hypercorrection could even be, 'Sir, do you drop your aitches?' Answer: 'Nah, I don't do haitches.')

I'd like just to mention the 'home counties'. I was never quite sure about the Home Counties, as when I was very young, in my ignorance, I conflated it with the 'BBC Home Service', the national 'radio station' broadcasting from 1939 until 1967 – when it became BBC Radio 4!

Of course, the Home Counties are those surrounding London, within their 1889 borders; think of Berkshire, Buckinghamshire, Essex, Hertfordshire, Kent, Surrey and Sussex. These are some, but not all, of the Home Counties. Oxfordshire and Cambridgeshire are sometimes included – as it would not do to leave them out.

What could be more apt to describe the Home Counties than to rely on this quote from a 1987 reference book. They are 'inhabited on the whole by nice, comfortable, and conformist middle-class people'.[1] The characteristics of a dwelling in the Home Counties were described as, 'a comfortable plasticized commuterland with respectable villas and neatly mown lawns interspersed with patches of mild scenery'.[2]

Could the subject of the following live in the Home Counties, one 'Blossom', featured in a TV documentary on 'Benefits Britain'? I think it was in the same programme, but I couldn't be sure. One female friend said, 'When you was in a coma, he was right there for you. It takes *a special kind of bloke to hang around* after something like that.' When I heard that, I wondered what kind of lady 'Blossom' might be. Your friends are not expected to hang around if they find you in a coma!

Blossom was quite lovely in her discussion of an operation she had had, the purpose of which I cannot remember. 'With me, d'you know what, I worried about being sick in the theatre, cos they're sterile, aren't they?' She got the results of her surgery afterwards, but scanning the papers didn't know what they meant. 'You'd 'aves to be Stephen bloody 'Awkins [Hawking] to read these, bless 'im.'

Then there was a Lenor advert, advising that if you used Lenor, you could avoid 'bobb-el-ling' with your woollens.

Finally, a woman seeking 'sŭck-sess', living on benefits. She 'couldn't afford them bullets' (reference to the Nutribullet blender/juicer). She was living 'the 'igh life' nevertheless, and was going on 'a 100-mile round trip to see a psychic in Blackpool', who would advise on her future career. 'When the psychic said to me, "you're goin' up, up, up", I felt this great big weight liftin' off me shoulders. Now I can feel the energies coming back.'

## Blackpool v the sunny south

Dare I suggest that if you feel a great weight on your shoulders, trying to comprehend how to pronounce words, say them right, or nearly right, that you go to Blackpool?

Perhaps I have not been entirely truthful with this 'correction malarkey'. You see, my parents originated from the north. My mother and father were married on the 8th

June 1940, at Bispham parish church, still known as the 'Mother Church of Blackpool'. My mother's father was sent to work at the age of ten 'down the mines', but he made his way out soon after, and became a successful journalist. My grandmother was one of nine children, some of whom died in childhood. It wasn't even 'two up and two down', more like one up and one down.

My father's uncle Fred had the first model 'T' Ford in his street, probably the first car in the street too. My father's father gave him a gold watch and chain, just before embarking for America but, on the wharf or was it the quayside, he grabbed the watch back. He ran off with a barmaid to live in America.

My mother more or less lost her northern accent but was still tied to *Coronation Street* for most of her adult life. My father became a solicitor, a major in the war, on the general staff; he chose the law because he had read *The Forsyte Saga* when only fourteen, and wanted to create the world that Old Jolyon Forsyte lived in, with a house on the hill, like Robin Hill. He moved to southern England, and made sure no one would judge him for being from the north by speaking as a southerner, with only very occasional lapses into the northern vernacular, perhaps after a drink or two.

When the call-up for war came, men joined long queues to sign up. My father (still then in the north) had no option but to quit his job as assistant solicitor and town clerk of Blackpool. An official, for want of a better word, asked him, as he moved to the front of the queue,

'Education?' My father answered 'Private', which wasn't true, but on hearing his answer, the official waved him through, to the line for prospective officers.

So, after all that, I don't want to go to Blackpool. That's where, in those dark and poor tenements of Lancashire, I owe my life, at least the origin of it, although born 'in the sunny south'. When I visit my dentist, she says, 'Your genes are to blame, you'd been handed down bad genes from somewhere in the past.' I know why. My week teeth are an inheritance from the bleak past, and pronunciation would have been the last thing to consider or worry about in the scramble for life.

'For that reason, I'm out.' A familiar refrain, but I suppose one day I *might* jump on a train and retrace my roots. What I would find there has as much currency as my own but is no longer relevant. Things were *right* (or *reet*) *gradely* then (meaning really good) but that's now 'all under the bridge'. Fortunately, we all move into the future and the past does not tie us too closely, for that perhaps would not be altogether good.

But, *d'you know what*, I think I'd rather listen to Northern folk (not because I'm English) than First Minister Nicola Sturgeon, expatiating on the need to protect Scottish interests, and a new referendum on Scottish independence. '*Did you know*' that historian David Starkey's opinion of Nicola Sturgeon is that she is 'a fascinating figure, a woman of penetrating intelligence who lives in La-La land'?[3]

She is so determined to do anything and everything she can 'to protect Scottish interests'. We have free movement within the UK, not just the EU's single market (for now). I would quite like to see Edinburgh Castle, and fish for salmon on the Tay, but I'm in no particular hurry. A week's fishing for salmon and deer hunting can cost £6,500, the irony being that the landowners are unlikely to be Scottish.

## Who owns all the grouse moors?

It will be interesting to see what happens if Scotland ever becomes independent. Vast swathes of grouse moors, baronial estates and hunting lodges owned by absentee landlords, often with overseas trust company arrangements, English aristocrats (and even some recent Arab investors) have effectively 'sown up' land ownership in the Highlands for hundreds of years. It is an odd but true fact that the Royal Family could not survive without the working masses, which are among its most vociferously loyal supporters. To keep them happy, a series of carefully choreographed events are laid on as sideshows for the faithful. The wrangling of unions and political parties nicely exempts royalty and leaves their enormously privileged positions unscathed and out of reach, leaving them free to invest even more in their large estates and put up rents every three years. They are very powerful landlords, as is the fiefdom of the National Trust.

Just over 500 people own half the land in Scotland. The Queen through the Crown Estate holds nearly 100,000 acres over four large estates in Scotland. Land reform is well overdue. (Prince Charles's Duchy Estate in Cornwall owns more than 130,000 acres in 23 or more counties (land, buildings, quarries, shorelines, etc.), with 13,000 of those in Cornwall) and is worth more than £1bn, and provides an income of some £20m.) Charging the Royal Family rent for Balmoral Castle or a compulsory purchase order adapted to fit new Scottish laws would really set the cat among the pigeons.

# CHAPTER ELEVEN

*'Reet gradely' – extract from a poem by William Barnes – British English (BrE) and American English (AmE) word differences – Tooting Bec – when Kennedy was shot*

To THROW A SPANNER in the works, and send the pronunciation pundits packing, let's look for a moment at some historical vernacular from the Dorset poet, William Barnes (1801–1886). It seems that the first recorded instance of throwing a spanner into the gears and pistons of an engine comes from P.G. Wodehouse's *Right Ho, Jeeves*, published in 1934.

There really isn't much difference between it and other British dialects of earlier times, including the northern 'reet gradely'. I was going to use the derogatory slang phrase, 'that northern shower' for a person or group considered slack, untidy or lazy. Why favour William Barnes (I live in Dorset) over the *reet gradely* lot up north? Personally, I never liked Barnes's poetry; it was far too parochial for my liking. The difference between Barnes and Keats, say, was the difference between a pit pony and an Arab thoroughbred. I think this shows how what we are used to affects our perceptions of ourselves, even our identities. Accents are personal. One should tread carefully.

Or tread softly, as in W.B. Yeats' poem, 'The Cloths of Heaven': 'Had I the heavens' embroidered cloths, / Enwrought with golden and silver light, / The blue and the dim and the dark cloths... / I have spread my dreams under your feet; / Tread softly because you tread on my dreams.'[1]

This Barnes extract is from *Poems of Rural Life in Common English*, published in 1866. It's title is 'Hay-Meaken'. It's not common English now.

> 'Tis merry ov a zummer's day,
> Where vo'k be out a-meäkèn hay;
> Where men an' women, in a string,
> Do ted or turn the grass, an' zing,
> Wi' cheemèn vaïces, merry zongs, A-tossèn o'
> their sheenèn prongs...'

Perhaps a few old men from Dorset would comprehend all of the above but the world has moved on. Giant combine harvesters patrol endless hedgeless spaces, and the 'shining prongs' have all gone rusty by now, but you might find one turning up on *Bargain Hunt*, where some avid buyers fuss and croon over such rustic 'heritage bygones'.

# Some British English (BrE) and American English (AmE) words

It could be said that American speakers throw in their own spanners (actually they call them 'wrenches') as, not only do they pronounce (and spell) many words differently with their version of 'American English', they also have words that English speakers would not recognise without a little practice. Oscar Wilde was always good or a 'dab hand' (expert or skilled at something) with quotes: 'We have really everything in common with America nowadays, except, of course, the language.' This includes pronouncing the word 'glacier'; here it can be glăcier or glācier, with the former preferred (but glācially) but the Americans have their own ideas: they might call it 'glay-sir' or 'glay-shir'.

Of hundreds of examples, I have selected just a few. Personally, I love tomah-toes but am not quite so keen on toe-may-toes. Why go to all the trouble of asking for a diaper (dye-per) when you simply want a nappy? The idea was to list some British English (BrE) words with their American English (AmE) equivalents but let's not forget the Americans need help too, in explaining the peculiarities of English in the UK.

Take the word 'trump'. In the US and UK, I'm fairly sure the main meaning refers to the 'trump card' in one of the four suits where players choose a 'trump card', one that will be worth more in a game.

In the UK and the US, one may also trump someone at the last hurdle – to 'come up trumps' – to succeed when success seems unlikely.

In the UK a 'trump' is a word that has been euphemistically used to refer to what is politely known as 'breaking wind'; in the US children are told not to 'toot'. I'm not sure what an American would make of Tooting Bec.

Does it really matter that an 'agony aunt' is an 'advice columnist', aluminium is aluminum or an aubergine is an eggplant? No, but it's fun to know. No doubt our US friends will laugh at us for calling fish sticks 'fish fingers'. Just as my mirth when considering an '*egg*plant'!

| | |
|---|---|
| baking tray | cookie sheet |
| bank holiday | legal holiday |
| bottom drawer | hope chest |
| courgette | zucchini |
| current account | checking account |
| danger money | hazard pay |
| double cream | heavy cream |
| fish finger | fish stick |
| flick knife | switchblade |
| green fingers | green thumb |
| grill | broil |
| homely | homey |
| jumble sale | rummage sale |
| loudhailer | bullhorn |
| lucky dip | grab bag |
| mangetout | snow pea |

| | |
|---|---|
| noughts and crosses | tic-tac-toe |
| paddling pool | wading pool |
| plough | plow |
| pushchair | stroller |
| rowing boat | rowboat |
| silencer (for car) | muffler |
| skipping rope | jump rope |
| slowcoach | slowpoke |
| swede | rutabaga |
| terrace house | row house |
| ticket tout | scalper |
| titbit | tidbit |
| waistcoat | vest |
| zebra crossing | crosswalk |

In the US, it's 'a tempest in a teapot' but when having a cup of Earl Grey at home in the UK, and an unnecessary row kicks off, it's 'a storm in a teacup'.

But what unites us is greater than what divides us.

Growing up, there was nothing quite as glamorous and so much fun as going to the local 'Tivoli' cinema to see an American film. It was escapism at its young best, with Marlon Brando filling the screen with his brooding, unforgettable charisma in *One-Eyed Jacks* or *On the Waterfront*. The day Kennedy was shot in Dallas, I remember too, like everyone else, where I was at the time, and the girl I was walking with on a sidewalk, I mean pavement, in my home town.

# CHAPTER TWELVE

*Received Pronunciation (RP) – Estuary English –
CAT theory of communication – John Betjeman –
renowned phonetician John Wells – girls and boys'
names to avoid – some Irish, Scottish and Welsh given
names – Prince Charles and 'splendid' – 'hedgehog
super highway' using Joanna Lumley's Garden Bridge –
Professor Higgins and Eliza Doolittle meet at art gallery*

I T'S NOW FULL CIRCLE as we tackle what is still considered
'a thorny issue': Received Pronunciation (RP). Just
think (or 'tink' as the Irish say) what some young people
had to do to escape the label: disguising their 'posh' accents
by pretending to have evolved nearer the Thames estuary!
Ashamed to call a spade a spade using their own accent!
'Ere mate, are you callin' that a spoide or a spade?' Any discussion of RP now has to include connections with other
forms of speech, such as 'Estuary English'.

The Thames estuary 'begins' in south-west London at
Teddington, with a foothold in Ham. If you've ever wondered how fast the tidal flow is, perhaps as you peer over
the parapet in Victoria Tower Gardens, it can reach eight

miles per hour. In this spot, spread your imaginative wings for many miles outside London, and nearby home counties around London, principally those of Kent and Essex (but also including Surrey, Hertfordshire, and of course London) and you will get an idea of the reach or spread of 'Estuary English' (EE). This form of speech sits somewhere in the middle between RP and cockney.

As a brief diversion, how many know the origin of the quote below?

> The sun set; the dusk fell on the stream, and lights began to appear along the shore...Lights of ships moved in the fairway – a great stir of lights going up and down. And farther west on the upper reaches the place of the monstrous town was still marked ominously on the sky, a brooding gloom in sunshine, a lurid glare under the stars.

A celebrated author knew of this area, as 'one of the dark places on the earth'. He lived close to the Essex marshes. In his book,[1] he describes this part of the Thames as being the river where great adventures in exploration began, with ships and crew sailing out to colonise the world. In earlier times the place had itself been colonised by the Romans. A new colonisation is well under way. It has been argued that EE may eventually replace RP in the south-east.[2] EE is said to be a lower middle class accent, not cockney working class, and is also sometimes used by the middle classes. There is little 'aitch-dropping' but users may use glottal stops (as in bu'er for butter and 'bu'on' for button), if they feel like it, surprisingly not though in slow speech. As an example of an Essex working class EE accent, look to Russell Brand.

Among what's left of RP speakers, there is a move towards EE or mockney, as a means of 'blending in', in the south-east and elsewhere. It also fits in as being more relaxed, less formal, and less exclusive compared with traditional RP (e.g. from the Chelsea and Kensington set). It gels very well with less rigid dress codes for many business occasions, such as open-necked shirts, no ties.

The shame of it! I feel I know what Will Shakespeare would have done. As a true 'man for all seasons', he would have spoken exactly as he preferred and not bowed down or shrunk away, ashamed of his voice or accent. I mean I doubt he would have altered anything for the sake of it, to suit fashion's whims. To be sure, some of his plays (in good old Black Country accent!) were adapted to fit the times but if you met the man in the street, I think he would be true to himself and speak just as he wished, without artifice or pretence.

The counterargument holds, however. It's a process of adaptation, which is always ongoing, and is perhaps to be welcomed in order to escape from what Melvyn Bragg called 'the intimidating pressures of the control dialect of English society'.[3] For context, Melvyn Bragg was referring to the accent of the then Director-General of the BBC, Greg Dyke as 'nearer to Chaucer than Prince Charles', and that his (Dyke's) accent 'announces itself unaffected' by the perceived elite's 'control dialect', with the inference (Mr Bragg is a left-winger or to use a more polite term, a socialist) that the ruling classes use RP as a means to 'control' (or otherwise coerce or subdue) the working masses. On second thoughts, I think Shakespeare would have approved.

A friend of mine (the one who reported on 'reggerlay'ers', see p. 121) has the habit of 'descending into the vernacular' at 'gigs' and seedy bars, where the beer constantly swills over the floor, by pretending to speak like those near him. He felt this would make them more comfortable. *'Awight mate? 'Ow's it goin'?'* If asked when he was next going on holiday, he might reply with something like, *'I dunno mate. I dunno. Could be soon, could be soona, moight be next year, the way fings are goin' like.'*

I used to stand next to him, horror struck with the acting audacity, the condescension, the supreme patronising, from someone who counted Russian princesses and nobility in his background, as well as a prestige boarding school that was once the grand country home of Lord Portman. The very house he grew up in, in Moscow, is now a national museum. It's his choice, however.

*'A man has to say what he says. There's no breaking the mould…'*

Yet, there is an explanation, first put forward by Howard Giles, a professor of Communication at the University of California, Santa Barbara in the 1990s. He developed an idea known as the CAT theory, or Communication

Accommodation Theory. It describes two main processes we engage in when socialising. There is 'convergence', when people interact with each other they will adjust their speech, vocal patterns and gestures 'to accommodate to others'.[4] The purpose is to reduce social differences 'through their communicative behaviours'.

Conversely, there is 'divergence', which is when individuals accentuate their speech and non-verbal differences.

*''Ere, Guv, did you just call a black cab?'*

*'I most certainly did, young man. Shall I hop on board?'*

However, sometimes when individuals try convergence to try to mix in, they can 'end up over-accommodating, and despite their good intentions their convergence can be seen as condescending'.[5]

RP is now spoken by only about 2 per cent of the British population! You wouldn't exactly guess so from listening to a variety of pundits on BBC Two (originally styled BBC2) and Radio 4. The word 'received' refers, like the phrase 'received wisdom', to what was then considered to be 'accepted' or 'approved'. This accent has been known by various names including 'Oxford English' and 'BBC English' but is now mainly referred to as 'Standard English'. RP has been subdivided into several categories but now its main labels are Conservative RP, mainstream RP, and Contemporary RP spoken by younger people.

Traditionally, RP was the everyday speech of families in (mainly) Southern England where the men were educated as boarders at prestigious public schools (e.g. Eton,

Harrow, Rugby, Winchester, etc.), completing their education at the Universities of Oxford and Cambridge. The great secret of RP was the idea that the education they received would subsequently provide *not a single clue as to the speaker's origin or county* they had lived in as children, although an RP accent did give a wealth of clues as to class and social background.

I have to say I am relieved that the 'old RP' of 50 years ago has virtually disappeared for ever. The Queen has demonstrably modified her accent over the past 50 years, no longer saying 'rah-hly' (or 'rarely') for really and pronouncing 'land', for example, more like today's 'lend'. The 'cawst' of the upkeep of royal estates is still there but now it's simply 'cŏst'.

Other aged RP speakers still insist on 'Keen-yah' for 'Ken-ya' and, why, only *today*, I heard one very well spoken lady, in a quiet country pub in Dorset refer to the landlady having visited 'Aws-tralia' the year before. She was a bit strange as she fed her two 'Scotty dogs' chunks of raw carrot from a plastic container.

There was even URP, or Upper Received Pronunciation, favoured in the past by aristocrats. Noel Coward used it. The man responsible for insisting RP be used by presenters in the BBC in the 1920s was its director general, Lord Reith. Today, BBC English is seen as 'correct' but allows far more variation in its use of regional accents (it positively thrives on them).

Because the ruling and privileged classes continued in this vein, RP speech became the voice of 'The

Establishment', contributing to its prestige and socially exclusive status, especially in London among the metropolitan elite. (It did not matter that much to fail one's degree – John Betjeman was sent down from Magdalen College without a degree. His tutor, C.S. Lewis, considered him 'an idle prig'. He did however make Poet Laureate in 1972 and in 2011 the University of Oxford awarded him an honorary Doctorate of Letters, a rare honour, as it made him 'one of its 100 most distinguished members from ten centuries').[6] Geographically, the accent could trace its roots to the 'south-east Midlands', for which read, loosely, London, Oxford and Cambridge.

The most notable linguist/dialectologist observer today is probably John C. Wells.[7] It's more correct to describe him as a distinguished 'British phonetician'. He has written much on the subject, and bravely lists some people he considers to be RP speakers, including the British Royal Family, David Attenborough, David Cameron, Boris Johnson, and Justin Welby, the Archbishop of Canterbury. This seems a rather illustrious but easily identifiable list.

Listening to a TV clip on the chef Keith Floyd, I realized you could describe his accent as RP but why? He had working class parents named Sydney and Winnifred; they lived in a small council house in Somerset. Floyd's parents made enormous efforts to send him to the independent Wellington School. His education probably nurtured his confident style, ably assisted by a glass or two of red.

Listening to the *Sun*'s political editor recently, who 'pops up' on TV fairly regularly, I thought he's quite well spoken, with a good face. What's he doing at the *Sun*? Before Edinburgh University, he went to the same secondary school as Siegfried Sassoon, John Betjeman, and the Duchess of Cambridge. Of course, he's an Old Malburian, £33k a year Marlborough College. I almost forgot to mention his name: Tom Newton Dunn. Those schools can even get you a job on the *Sun*!

Just like going to Gordonstoun School, whose alumni include the Duke of Edinburgh, Prince Charles, Charles Kennedy, William Boyd, and the *Daily Mail*'s political editor-at-large, Isabel Oakeshott whose easy-going, authoritative style assuredly owes something to the school whose motto is *Plus est en vous*, 'There is more in you.'

(Care is advised when choosing a name for your child. Examples of not the best choices [from dozens] being Dwaine, Kyle, Tyler, and Wayne for boys and Chelseigh, Cortnee, Kayleigh, and Paige for girls.)

If you are Welsh or have some connection with Wales you could choose a Welsh boys' name like Alun, Caradog, Carwyn, Dafydd, Griff, Gruffydd, Gwili, Ioan, Llwyd, Madog, Pawl, Owen, Phylip, Selwyn, Tomos, or Wmffre (the Welsh name for Humphrey!).

If Scottish, there's Aengus (Celtic for Angus), Aillig (person from a rocky location), Ailbeart (Gaelic for Albert), Ailean (Alan), Baldie (from Archibald), Beiste, ('the beast'), Blair (no comment), Niall ('champion'), Ross, Torquil, and so on.

If Irish, there's Conchobhar, Dermot, Diarmuid, Dougal, Murtagh, Oisin (pron. oh-sheen), Riordan, Seamus (James), Tadhg (Timothy), or Ultan ('an Ulsterman'). Perhaps some *might* take their inspiration for naming a child from Father Ted, Father Dougal, and Father Jack. Tread carefully. (Should anyone outlandishly, and dare I say mistakenly, want to follow the charmingly inept Mrs Doyle, her Christian name is believed to be 'Joan'. One can understand anyone choosing 'Joan' if in memory of Jeanne d'Arc, the Maid of Orleans but if after Mrs Doyle, a touch of the Emerald Isle must have got into your tea!)

## More on Estuary English

As mentioned earlier, linguistics is an academic subject beyond the scope of *The Pocket Book of (Proper) English Pronunciation*. I mean, for example, *did you know* that Estuary English can be characterised by such features as:

- Foot–strut split
- *L*-vocalisation
- T glottalisation
- Trap–bath split
- *Yod*-coalescence
- Various kinds of vowel changes
- Vowel mergers before the dark /l/…
- Wholly-holy split

*Note*: some *th*-fronting is appearing. This means pronouncing the 'th' in words like 'think' as fink. Also 'v' sounds for the 'th' in words like 'brother'.

If making a study of EE, you also need to know about consonant phonemes, and words like affricative, fricative, approximant, glottal reinforcement, creaky voice, allophones and monophthongs, diphthongs and triphthongs, and the BATH vowel (yes, it *is* to do with pronouncing the 'a' in 'bath' and similar sounding words, known as 'the BATH set'.[8] Other terms in phonology (the sounds of speech) include words like alveolar, dental, glottal, labial, palatal, post-alveolar, and velar...

## Hedgehog super highway

I think it's best to round off this chapter here, 'prorogue' it for a while. In fact, I think it's a *splendid* idea. The word splendid, which means 'brilliant, fine, shining, magnificent' is a favoured RP word (at least I think it is). Prince Charles uses it often. Its popularity among the RP classes has never really wavered, and it remains a potent kind of 'class signifier'. I couldn't say I am keen on 'frightfully splendid', as that sounds a bit too much Joanna Lumley(-ish), if her Garden Bridge ever gets built.

(According to Plymouth Sutton and Devonport MP, Oliver Colvile, the bridge could become 'a welcome home amid the bridge's trees and greenery' – for hedgehogs.[9] He would like a 'hedgehog habitat' to be created there. The Tory MP said the new bridge had the potential to become a 'hedgehog super highway'. That's about £200 million to make a hedgehog super highway – rather than more pedestrian culverts and hedgehog alleyways. Tramps could also find bases under trees and shrubs, and the entrepreneurial ones might throw a line over, under cover of darkness, to catch their breakfast. In time, a connecting 'super highway hedgehog route' might join up with Tower Bridge, until the bridge lifts. What a great way to catch and count hedgehogs as they slide off.)

Splendid it seems is not such a common word everywhere. Imagine two people staring at anything you care to imagine, perhaps a painting in Tate British or the National Gallery, which *is* simply splendid.

Prof. Higgins: *'That's really rather good, in fact it's quite splendid.'*

Eliza Doolittle: *'Aw, that ain't 'arf bad, in fact Professor 'Iggins, it's a bit of awight, init?'*

# POSTSCRIPT

*Inclusiveness — 'upspeak (the high rising terminal) — a note on alma maters — sounds of speech — some faux pas — Riesling or Reisling — lunch or dinner? — U and non-U examples — the trap–bath split — serendipity with words — more on dress codes for men — a 'double' apocryphal story — more that unites us than divides — 'tongues are beautiful' — au revoir to the mischievious athalete and the grumpy duck!*

WELL, SOONER OR LATER the 'pedant' has to give in. It's all *about* inclusiveness now. Why, this morning I heard a woman, a reverend in the Church of England, saying just the same on TV. This was the Rev Sally Hitchiner, who runs the LGBT support group, Diverse Church. Everybody should be able 'to step up to the plate', which (*don't you know?*) is a baseball term. (A notable 'pedant-puncturer' is the British journalist and writer, Oliver Kamm. He writes a column in *The Times* on English usage.)

All minorities of whatever sexual 'persuasion', all migrants, refugees, neighbours, races, friends, even your long-lost aunt, all have the right 'to partake' in this great glorious togetherness – even the first Anglican bishop, Bishop Nicholas Chamberlain, who has come out as being gay. As long as he stays within the bishops' guidelines, and is 'celibate', he can openly live with his partner with the blessing of the Church. What is needed from the Church is a precise definition of 'celibate' as applied to gay clergy, so that all understand what is involved. Meanings of words can take on so many hues. People can hide behind words too.

The meaning of words changes too. To be sure (a favourite Irish expression) originally 'booty' was a neutral word referring to stolen goods, plunder seized in wartime or by force or piracy. A funny cartoon in *The Times* (4 October 2016) actually refers to its real meaning – and its slang version (for buttocks). There's the usual couple discussing breakfast news with a newspaper; the headline is £10m KARDASHIAN ROBBERY, and the caption is 'Quite a big booty'.

As an admittedly bizarre aside, a recent news clip showed Freddie Mercury's house where he lived as a child, which had a blue plaque proudly affixed to the front wall. The announcer said, 'He was living in a terraced house at the time.' I thought how rare it is to hear, 'He was living in a detached house at the time.' The subject might have been living in a castle or a caravan but rarely in a detached house. Of course, it's all about the climb from humble beginnings. There are some delightful terraced houses. They must get such a bad press because some have been linked or associated with the working class, an unfair slight.

Asides over, after that a smart young Irish executive by the name of 'Dean Doyle' was interviewed on TV, saying that Iran was opening up to tourism. He said there were great places to see in Iran, lots of scenery and impressive mountains, and not just the usual things but places 'like Per-sop-elis and Isha-pan' too. *'Don't you know?'* I felt like saying. 'It's Per-sep-olis (Persepolis), not Per-sop-elis, and that immortal and gloriously romantic city is Is-pha-haan (Isfāhān) and not Isha-păn.

## Upspeak (or the high rising terminal)

What do you think of 'upspeak'? I find it slightly annoying. It's popular with Australians and New Zealanders. Generally, it's not a good idea to upspeak if applying for any professional job.

The upspeak speaker's intonation rises inexorably towards the end of a statement, like a Swiss train trying to pull itself up a steep gradient. The annoying part is that it's used (the rising intonation) in a statement that is not necessarily a question. Ask an Aussie the way to a road near Earls Court: 'Go down *to the corner*, and then *follow it round*, and then go on *a bit more* until you see *a big white building in front of you.*' The italics are for the rising bits. By the time the Aussie stops speaking, you're sort of left hanging there, waiting for some sort of question, or finality, that never happens. Linguists have a technical term for upspeak; it's called the 'high rising terminal'. *'Hey, do me a favour fella, could you cut down a bit on the high rising terminal?'*

However, it's not as annoying as someone who stands next to you, carefully watching your mouth while you are talking, and then jumps in to say the last few words of the sentence for you. Without making a so-called sexist remark, women seem better at this peculiar facility.

## A note on alma maters

The use of 'nourishing mothers' to indicate or illustrate someone's educational background, as happens in *The Pocket Book of (Proper) English Pronunciation*, is by way of a little extra 'elucidation', and is not meant to be interpreted any differently. The mention of alma maters is not consistent (e.g. not all persons mentioned herein get an alma mater/education mention).

Until now, neither did the Archbishop of Canterbury, but since he gets a mention in the RP section (see p. 149), one might as well add his alma maters: Eton College, Trinity College, Cambridge; St John's College, Durham.

Justin Welby, who has acknowledged he can 'speak in tongues' (known as 'glossolalia') and regards himself as a bit of 'a spiritual magpie' was once told by the then Bishop of Kensington, the late John Hughes: 'There is no place for you in the Church of England',[1] an example of Cowper's dictum, 'God moves in a mysterious way.'[2] It's a bit like pronunciation really. You're never quite sure what to expect!

Eton produces personalities that seem to rise effortlessly to the top, like cream (or even floats on the top like double cream). Of the 53 UK prime ministers (2016),

19 went to Eton, 7 Harrow and 6 Westminster School. Of these 27 went to Oxford, 14 to Cambridge. Eton and Christ Church, Oxford is a favourite route (9 PMs). A small number went to grammar schools (e.g. Harold Wilson, Theresa May). Eleven prime ministers attended one of the four Inns of Court (Gray's Inn, Inner Temple, Lincoln's Inn, Middle Temple), training as barristers. Two, Wellington (Eton) and Churchill (Harrow), completed officer training at military academies. Hugh Fearnley-Whittingstall and Bear Grylls are also Eton alumni.

*Note:* Sometimes more than one 'alma mater' is given, in which case, please read 'alma maters' though the singular is used.

## Sounds of speech

*Phonology* is the linguistic term used to describe the sounds made in speech. It describes, or attempts to describe, the structure of speech sounds, and how these combine to create all the magnificent meanings that come from the words, phrases and sentences we use. The smallest unit of sound that amounts to something is called a 'phoneme'. The English alphabet has only 26 letters but there are about 44 phonemes used in 'Standard English', one of numerous dialects.

As for the universality of language, there are even today over 6500 languages in use although just under one third have fewer than 1000 speakers. More than 300 different languages are spoken in London. (For the record, 'speaking in tongues' involves no known languages. It is therefore entirely unintelligible and gibberish, though believers suggest it is 'God's spirit' speaking through them.)

Perhaps of more import is that every child in very early childhood has the ability to 'sound' any of the sounds 'needed to create all the words used in any world language'! That is a kind of infant glossolalia unique to the human species. The ability to make these sounds slowly erodes as the mother tongue takes hold. Later, these 'phonemes' become inaccessible or simply 'lost' and have to be consciously re-learned if a young adult wishes to learn another language. Infants are therefore 'hard-wired' to make any sound from any language they are born in to, so perhaps the story of Tarzan learning to converse with apes isn't so far-fetched after all.

## Some faux pas

Thankfully, the old style faux pas are going out of use although new ones are always being invented. Old style, for example, was to say you've been 'horse riding' as 'riding' sufficiently conveys meaning enough, and anyway what else would you be riding but a horse? This must mean it's okay to say you've been camel riding or dolphin riding in countries where camels and dolphins are not indigenous. The same sort of logic is presumably used in Bahrain or countries where camels are raced, where it must be a kind of local faux pas to say you've been 'camel riding', since everyone at one time rode around on camels. [I realise this argument is improbable and deeply flawed.] Many people in desert countries now ride on dune buggies, and actually chase camels, as does Saudi billionaire Turki Bin Abdullah in a six-wheel Mercedes G63.]

Many people have severe lacunae when it comes to knowing anything much about wine. Mention a Trockenbeerenauslese and you will most probably be met with a blank stare of considerable confusion.

The fact that it's more expensive than most white wines has nothing to do with it. You can buy a 2002 Nackenheimer Rothenberg Riesling Trockenbeerenauslese Gunderloch for about £180 a half bottle or £1600 a case: a white wine dried on the vine (trocken/dry) (although sweeter than most) with berries/beeren (grapes) left, picked later/left out longer (auslese = selected late harvest) to acquire noble rot (botrytis) – the grapes so shrivelled as to look like raisins. Spätlese wines are made from late-harvest grapes. Auslese means made from selected extra-ripe grapes so they have higher sugar content. There is also Eiswein, when the grapes are picked literally with ice on them/frozen. The correct order for Qualitätswein mit Prädikat, that's quality German white wine with 'special attributes/styles' is: Kabinett (delicate, crisp, green), Spätlese, Auslese, Beerenauslese, Eiswein and Trockenbeerenauslese. The names of wines can really be a minefield sometimes when it comes to 'saying it right'. I got caught out this evening by a 'Vosne-Romanée. I had the acute accent right but did not figure that 'Vosne' is pronounced 'vone' as in bone!

Luckily, there's a website for this: http://www.dummies.com/food-drink/drinks/wine/how-to-pronounce-french-wine-names/.

Of course, further detail is 'outwith' (a Scottish English word) the scope or purview of this book, and even the foregoing is a bit of an indulgence. The trouble is so many people, especially young women looking for white wine ask if there is any Rise-ling instead of Rees-ling (Riesling) and have they any Shab-liss (or even Chab-liss) rather than Shăb-lee (Chablis). 'Prosecco', in contrast, is a breeze. On the other hand, a Waitrose wine member of staff asked me if I wanted any 'Sav-ee-non blanc' rather than 'Sau-vign-non' (Sauvignon)

Choosing the right word is still important so as 'not to give the game away' *or* let others know they are considered social outsiders. When I was growing up, if relaxing in the drawing room, one either simply lay down on a rug near the fire or sprawled comfortably on a couch. Not many other people's houses that I knew had couches. Many had sofas and a few had settees. The word 'settee' engendered a kind of social response (in the family) akin to a dog's coat bristling at the sign of an unwelcome guest. People had settees up north. The only settees found in the south of England were in the houses of people who had moved from the north to the south, taking their settees with them.

There are lists of accents, as in the most disliked to the most liked but people prefer their own accents, even if they know it's not high up on the list of 'most liked accents'. They get used to the familiarity of their own voices; say 'Bath' with a long 'a' to some northerners and they will either burst into fits of laughter at such a stupid-sounding word or recoil in amazement that any living person could make such a preposterous sound. As with accents, it's the same for people's belongings. Some love the idea of a settee and others would not go near one.

It used to be infra dig to say 'serviette' (unless actually in France) instead of (table) 'napkin', and still is. I often wish there was another word. I can't say I'm too fond of the word 'napkin', which to me implies a rolled up, heavily starched cloth in a silver napkin holder; it seems too unnecessarily grand a word for everyday use and a serviette is still considered as shudderingly non-U by some, in the same way that U-speakers have lunch in the day and dinner in the evening; a meal rather less than dinner is sometimes called supper; non-U speakers have their 'dinner' at lunchtime and their 'evening meal' or sometimes 'tea' in the evening. 'I'll go *mash* (brew) the tea' is East Midlands English dialect (think Yorkshire, Leicestershire), and 'If you don't hurry up abou' t'it, I'll get all *mardy* on yer' (grumpy/moody).

One can't ask for a 'napkin' in a working-class café where you've just gone for egg and chips with brown or red sauce. If you do, expect staff to say something like, 'D'you mean serviette, love? You want a serviette? You're a bit mischievious, aren't you? Did you want brown or red sauce? We've got brown, red or yellow sauce, that's mustard.' 'Do you have any HP sauce?' 'What? I'm not some kind of athalete; go down the shops in five seconds, an' get yer HP sauce. No, we only 'ave brown sauce 'ere love, an' red, an' yellow too – if you feel like it.'

The man responsible for the terms U and non-U (Upper class and non-Upper class), first used in 1954 in an academic paper, 'Upper-Class English Usage', was Alan Ross, a British Professor of Linguistics at Birmingham University. His original work, especially the phrase U and non-U, was reprised, borrowed in fact by the novelist Nancy Mitford.

To be thoroughly U one must still have a pudding and not a sweet. Puddings are such heartily British fare, often full of suet, sponge, sultanas and custard. I find nothing wrong with 'dessert' but no doubt somebody somewhere objects.

It is still true that you should go racing, if you can, at Asc't and not As-COT. Here are just a few more examples. It doesn't do to dwell too much because much of this matters less today (thank goodness).

| Okay | Not okay |
|------|----------|
| loo, lavatory, bog | piss house, toilet, crapper, WC |
| what? sorry? | pardon? excuse me? |
| get pregnant | fall pregnant, or expecting* |
| grandma, granny | nan[†], nana |

| | |
|---|---|
| breakfast, lunch or dinner | go out for a meal |
| pudding | sweet, dessert |
| smart (posh okay if jokingly) | posh |
| how d'you do | pleased to meet you |
| hello | alright?[‡] |

*Note:* Going to the loo or lavatory (LAvuhtree) is perhaps still marginally politer than 'toilet' although Kate Middleton has been overheard asking for one, and 'toilet' is readily recognisable as a kind of lingua franca all over the world. Lavatory has always seemed to me a vaguely silly word, or at least one that Patricia Routledge as Hyacinth Bouquet would prefer, in her aspirational lower middle class way. Asking for the WC (water closet) doesn't go down well – although I have asked for 'the WC' in restaurants sometimes. It's perfectly well understood and I felt comfortable with it. Why bother to say 'LA-vuh-tree' to a migrant worker in a pizza parlour? Is it about context? In a rustic pub, it's fine to ask for 'the Gents'. In some pubs, if you quaintly ask for 'the LA-vuh-tree', the probable answer might be, 'Yer wot?'

The Americans always euphemistically ask for 'the bathroom', even though not taking a bath.

\* Not very nice slang phrases for pregnant are: 'In the family way', 'a bun in the oven' or 'up the duff'.

[†] Not the pronunciation of naan (bread), which rhymes with Laugharne ('larn') in Wales, i.e. not made out of grannies.

‡ The working or lower classes constantly ask if you are 'alright?' It's very solicitous of them. However, in supermarkets, I keep getting asked if I am 'all right', that is, am I about to keel over, am I ill or not ill, is my mind in one piece? The only reply I seem to give lately is a reworking of *cogito, ergo sum*, said with an element of doubt: 'I *think* I'm all right.'

| Okay activities/phrases | Not so okay activities/phrases |
| --- | --- |
| Walking the spaniels, Labradors | Walking the pitbulls/Alsatians/ferrets |
| Making Seville marmalade | Driving to Tesco to buy Golden Shred |
| Going to the Albert Hall for Last Night of the Proms | Going to a Karaoke night |
| Sing in a choir | Chant on the football terraces |
| Shopping for Ketchup and HP | Shopping for red and brown sauce |
| Cross | Getting the 'ump |
| Tired | Knackered |
| Go racing | Go 'dahn the dogs' |
| Gourmet/gourmand | Champagne socialist (Tony Blair) |
| Toff/old sport/dear chap | Stuck-up, toffee-nosed git |
| Expert | Ponce |

| Goodbye | I'll just leave now*, cheery-bye, ta-ta, ta-ra |
| Nuisance | Arsehole |
| Really? | Get away! |

* When leaving, some people say, 'Bye now'. If they are already leaving then/at that moment, why say 'Bye *now*?' No one says, 'Bye in 15 minutes' or, 'Hello now' (not usually) when meeting up.

## What is the TRAP–BATH Split?

Is it a trap set out to catch the Mischievious Athalete? No! The TRAP vowel set includes words like trap, cat, bad, mat. In the north of England and Scottish English there isn't a Trap–Bath split! All Trap and Bath vowels are pronounced the same, with a short 'a'. This single feature of language divides much of the country, and could be considered divisive. It sets up a 'them and us' scenario – which works both ways. Other parts of the country also have variations, which can make classification hard.

The BATH vowel set includes words pronounced like bath, laugh, calf, staff, answer, graph, path, aunt. RP or Standard English, Cockney/Estuary English are accents with the Trap–Bath split.

So, in the north you might 'throw your b*a*d c*a*t and your *a*unt in the b*a*th' – all the 'a' vowels are short (no Trap–Bath split). But, in the RP parts of the south and east, you would 'throw your b*ă*d c*ă*t and your *ā*unt in the bāth'. That's two short 'a' vowels and two 'broad' or long 'a' vowels. Hence the Trap–Bath split down south and east. Another set is the FOOT–STRUT split (pronouncing words like put and putt differently).

What intrigue there is in the simple accent? One thinks of machinations – should that be 'mack-in-ations' or 'mash-in-ations'? Although I thought the first was 'right', and eschewed the '*mash*ination' pronunciation (too near to sausages and mash), both are correct. For the origin of this word, think of carefully contrived *machines* and scheming plots. Like so much else, online etymological dictionaries can be quickly looked up, e.g. www.etymonline.com.

As mentioned earlier, there's much more to linguistics than the Trap–Bath split. There's *l-vocalization* (milk bottle becomes more like 'miwk botoo'); *glottalling* (Gatwick is pronounced 'Ga'wick); *happY-tensing*; *yod coalescence*, etc. Plus many more vowel tables or lexical sets, named after a representative keyword, like the GOAT set (example words: soap, home, soul), and STRUT, FOOT, FACE, PALM, GOOSE, etc., etc. *To be honest*, I prefer to leave this to the experts.

## Serendipity with words

Having an interest in words leads to all kinds of serendipitous new discoveries. Just this morning I finally found out the meaning of 'persiflage', reminded myself of some 1920s ways of saying 'good-bye' (toodle pip, toodle oo) and was near mortified to learn that I never knew – in my entire life so far – how to pronounce cognoscenti (also conoscenti) properly! [At least I didn't say 'proply'.] What is worse, I thought I must have been a member of the cognoscenti myself for being able to pronounce it. (I also made a mistake for years when pronouncing Horace's great quote, *carpe diem* (seize the day!). The first word has nothing to do with carp of the fishing variety, it's car-pay diem.) My excuse is that perhaps there is a kind of Anglicised version about that's acceptable. Also the singular (not known before) is cognoscente – a person with an informed opinion or appreciation in a particular field, especially in the fine arts, as in a connoisseur (that's con-o-sir, not con-o-sewer).

*Cono-shenti!*

EmmaSaying.com says it loud and clear.[3] Lately by the way I have 'gone off' EmmaSaying, who is probably a computer algorithm rather than a real person. Firstly, I never forgave her for not getting 'almond' right (see p. 125); and secondly, when I listened to the way she pronounced 'bath',[4] I wanted to drown her in one. The word is sort of 'spat out' like verbal venom. It wouldn't be so bad if she gave the other pronunciation too. You know, the BATH set of vowels – see above. 'She' does make mistakes. I don't think she's too hot with 'minutiae', for instance. When it comes to that superbly languorous creature called a sloth, it can be *either* 'slŏth' or 'slōth'. Perhaps this allows a slŏthful slōth or a slōthful slŏth.

As for 'persiflage', it's a kind of humorous banter, light frivolous conversation or friendly teasing, a bit like 'joshing'. It's one of those words I 'knew' but didn't. It was easier in the past to put off looking up the meaning of a word; now you can just enter it on your phone and find dozens of answers offered, e.g. Wiktionary.

As well as phonetician John C. Wells, one must mention David Crystal, honorary Professor of Linguistics, University of Bangor. As an academic, linguist, public speaker and broadcaster, Professor Crystal has authored over one hundred books on phonetics and related topics. He became a Fellow of the British Academy in 2000.

Just as there are words to pronounce in a certain way (or not pronounce), there are also numerous dress codes – as there are dozens of accents in the UK. Tom Utley, for example, commented in the *Daily Mail* that, if looking for a city job, men should not wear *white* shirts at interview (too obvious), steer clear of 'loud' ties, and definitely not wear *brown* shoes.[5] If you have to wear brown shoes, make sure the trouser belt you wear is black. A 'proper' shirt does *not* have a chest pocket. Shirt pockets are for tradesmen and 'janitors'. Also never hang keys from your belt, or risk being mistaken for the odd-job man. Tattoos can also lose jobs; hidden below the neckline is suggested if you really must have one. The *Daily Mail* correspondent followed this with an assuredly apocryphal story told by his mother. She confided to him, on the subject of whether a man's jacket should have two side vents or one middle one, that one was a 'b****r's dilemma' and the other a 'b****r's delight', and *for the life of him*, he could not remember which was which. That's two apocryphal stories in one!

In late 2016 South Korea described the testing of North Korea's biggest bomb to date as 'maniacal recklessness'. The statement was picked up by news channels. I happened to be watching one, the newsreader said: 'Kim Jong-un's activities were described as may-knee-ack-al recklessness'. It just didn't sound right. I switched over. The next newsreader said, 'The man-EYE-accul, or try this again, the man-EYE-ăcul recklessness of Kim Jong-un...' So, you don't say the word with an initial 'maniac' after all. And EmmaSaying gets it right.[6]

The funny thing is that it is not the recklessness that is maniacal; it's Kim Jong-un himself who is the maniac. He is really what one would describe in the UK as 'a total nutter', and a nasty one too. He has murdered quite a lot of people, executing over 70 officials by firing squad, thrown an uncle alive into a cage containing 120 starving dogs, and blown up a political dissenter into a thousand pieces with an anti-aircraft gun. He is reported as saying to the man at the execution, 'I never want to see you again', which actually was impossible after the anti-aircraft gun blew him to smithereens (small fragments). I don't think I'd bother describing Jim Jong-un's behaviour as maniacal; I'd just call him *a maniac*. I see by mistake I typed Jim Jong-un; there's a new spoonerism here, which also implies something from a horror movie. I mean Jim Kong-un.

Why do Americans pronounce the silent 'h' in Anthony? (An-thu-knee or Ann-thuh (like duh) knee). Blame William Camden who, in the sixteenth century, claimed the name had a connection with the Greek for flower (*anthos*) or perhaps a small yellow bird, and stuck an 'h' in the name. This pronunciation and spelling soon became common in America but not in Britain. That explains why Shakespeare's play is *Antony and Cleopatra*.

Be careful not to put *'erbicides* on 'em. Really, the Americans love 'erbs like OREG-an-o (cf. British, or-eG-ANO). I have just heard a Kenyan chef on Channel 4 (Kiran Jethwa) talk about Mongolian lamb and 'papreeka' stew. I might, possibly, be prepared to forgive EmmaSaying as she agrees with me, that it's paprika with a short 'i' like 'PAPricka'. Luckily, I have already eaten my dinner (in case of doubt, I ate (that is 'et') in the evening about 7.30ish – *definitely* not lunchtime). Still on the subject of 'erbs, *did you know* that 'rosemary', which the Americans call *Rose Mary* (two distinct words), and we call 'ROSE-murree', in origin is nothing to do with either roses or the (virgin) Mary? It means 'dew of the sea', a pointer to the poetry (once called *poesy*) in words. Have you time to listen to the meaning of 'thyme'? Why put an 'h' in the word? In ancient Greece, it was *'thumon'*, from *'thuein'* (don't ask me why), and it meant 'to make a burnt offering' – 'that which goes up in smoke'. The idea behind burnt offerings was to give 'sweet savour' to the deity one worshipped. The gods or god could not *eat* the food offered in sacrifice but they might appreciate the smells from the burnt offering (including the fat) going up in smoke. Not many people make burnt offerings nowadays. *Imagine making one for Jonathan Ross or Lady Gaga – or Jeremy Corbyn or Theresa May or … … … insert name here!*

When I started writing this pocket book, I had a few dislikes of accents and certain pronunciations, to be sure some on a subconscious level. Things changed when I spoke to the girl from Liverpool, so animatedly positive and proud of her background, her city, all of which *made her belong*. I began to realise that 'tongues are beautiful'. Accents mean tribes, histories, differentiations. Our history is written notably in the *Anglo Saxon Chronicle*, the single most important historical source for the history and early development of English. Once there were 'thegns' pron. thanes (retainers, servants, freemen), ealdormen (elder men) and high-reeves (great stewards). The thanes became barons and then later, knights. To listen to how Anglo-Saxon was spoken is like entering another world, yet one with which we must have ancestral memories deep within us.

Perhaps there is more that unites us than divides us but accents divide, not unkindly, but serve to differentiate, and each person is strangely located within a tribe, a district, a village, a county, just by the way they pronounce their vowels. When Jesus spoke to his disciples, he didn't use the fine words of the King James Bible but spoke in Aramaic with a Galilean accent. Whether the Lord's Prayer was originally spoken in Jewish Aramaic or Syrian Aramaic I don't know but there is a certain enchantment, almost magic for the imagination to listen to the original. This example is sung[7] but if you can, try to find one which is spoken in Aramaic, not for any religious inference but simply to hear 'the tongue' (as it was then) in which it is pronounced.

Chimpanzees, our closest relatives, may have slightly different vocalisations from one area to another but they all 'speak chimp'. Humans are truly unique in having thousands of languages, tens of thousands of dialects and accents, so that's why I now say, 'tongues are beautiful'! You have to include accents and dialects too, a fortiori.

So, to conclude you can't really say, 'There's no going back…There's no breaking the mould.' It gets broken all the time, continually reshaped, like those pots of Omar Khayyam's, moulded and re-moulded, sometimes 'nearer to the heart's desire' and sometimes not, this language of ours, this English, this sweet English, and all the other languages, accents and dialects on earth, evolving with us regardless of whether we like it or not. It's something to celebrate: 'Vive les differences!'

And it's time to send *the mischievious athalete* on his way – and the grumpy (or cloomsy) duck too.

# APPENDIX 1

*'The Chaos' by Gerard Nolst Trenité, 1870–1946*

S OME FUN TO BE had trying to pronounce all these words as they should be pronounced. The words in italics in the first three verses may help you get started. I don't know much about the author but would not be surprised if he had a nervous breakdown after completing his poem.

## 'The Chaos' by Gerard Nolst Trenité, 1870–1946

Dearest *creature* in *creation*,
Study English pronunciation.
I will teach you in my verse
Sounds like *corpse*, *corps*, *horse*, and *worse*.
I will keep you, *Susy*, *busy*,
Make your *head* with *heat* grow *dizzy*.
*Tear* in eye, your dress will *tear*.
So shall I! Oh hear my *prayer*.

*Pray*, console your loving poet,
Make my coat look *new*, dear, *sew* it!
Just compare *heart*, *beard*, and *heard*,
*Dies* and *diet*, *lord* and *word*,
*Sword* and *sward*, *retain* and *Britain*.
(Mind the latter, how it's written.)
*Made* has not the sound of *bade*,
*Say-said*, *pay-paid*, *laid*, but *plaid*.

Now I surely will not *plague* you
With such words as *vague* and *ague*.
But be careful how you speak:
Say *break* and *steak*, but *bleak* and *streak*;
*Previous*, *precious*, *fuchsia*, *via*; Cloven, oven, how and low,
Script, receipt, show, poem, and toe.

Hear me say, devoid of trickery,
Daughter, laughter, and Terpsichore,
Typhoid, measles, topsails, aisles,
Exiles, similes, and reviles;
Scholar, vicar, and cigar,
Solar, mica, war and far;
One, anemone, Balmoral,
Kitchen, lichen, laundry, laurel;
Gertrude, German, wind and mind,
Scene, Melpomene, mankind.

Billet does not rhyme with ballet,
Bouquet, wallet, mallet, chalet.

Blood and flood are not like food,
Nor is mould like should and would.
Viscous, viscount, load and broad,
Toward, to forward, to reward.
And your pronunciation's OK
When you correctly say croquet,
Rounded, wounded, grieve and sieve,
Friend and fiend, alive and live.

Ivy, privy, famous; clamour
And enamour rhyme with hammer.
River, rival, tomb, bomb, comb,
Doll and roll and some and home.
Stranger does not rhyme with anger,
Neither does devour with clangour.
Souls but foul, haunt but aunt,
Font, front, wont, want, grand, and grant,
Shoes, goes, does. Now first say finger,
And then singer, ginger, linger,
Real, zeal, mauve, gauze, gouge and gauge,
Marriage, foliage, mirage, and age.

Query does not rhyme with very,
Nor does fury sound like bury.
Dost, lost, post and doth, cloth, loth.
Job, nob, bosom, transom, oath.
Though the differences seem little,
We say actual but victual.

Refer does not rhyme with deafer.
Foeffer does, and zephyr, heifer.
Mint, pint, senate and sedate;
Dull, bull, and George ate late.
Scenic, Arabic, Pacific,
Science, conscience, scientific.

Liberty, library, heave and heaven,
Rachel, ache, moustache, eleven.
We say hallowed, but allowed,
People, leopard, towed, but vowed.
Mark the differences, moreover,
Between mover, cover, clover;
Leeches, breeches, wise, precise,
Chalice, but police and lice;
Camel, constable, unstable,
Principle, disciple, label.

Petal, panel, and canal,
Wait, surprise, plait, promise, pal.
Worm and storm, chaise, chaos, chair,
Senator, spectator, mayor.
Tour, but our and succour, four.
Gas, alas, and Arkansas.
Sea, idea, Korea, area,
Psalm, Maria, but malaria.
Youth, south, southern, cleanse and clean.
Doctrine, turpentine, marine.

Compare alien with Italian,
Dandelion and battalion.
Sally with ally, yea, ye,
Eye, I, ay, aye, whey, and key.
Say aver, but ever, fever,
Neither, leisure, skein, deceiver.
Heron, granary, canary.
Crevice and device and aerie.

Face, but preface, not efface.
Phlegm, phlegmatic, ass, glass, bass.
Large, but target, gin, give, verging,
Ought, out, joust and scour, scourging.
Ear, but earn and wear and tear
Do not rhyme with here but ere.
Seven is right, but so is even,
Hyphen, roughen, nephew Stephen,
Monkey, donkey, Turk and jerk,
Ask, grasp, wasp, and cork and work.

Pronunciation – think of Psyche!
Is a paling stout and spikey?
Won't it make you lose your wits,
Writing groats and saying grits?
It's a dark abyss or tunnel:
Strewn with stones, stowed, solace, gunwale,
Islington and Isle of Wight,
Housewife, verdict and indict.

Finally, which rhymes with enough –
Though, through, plough, or dough, or cough?
Hiccough has the sound of cup.
My advice is to give up!

# ADDENDA

How many authors reach the end of a book they're writing, and then find something else to add that seems essential reading? Luckily, the final proofs are some way off, which means I can just squeeze in a few further points.

- The proofreader did warn me that I risked upsetting a few people from the north. When one thinks of the harm done to secular bloggers in Pakistan cut down with meat cleavers by religious fanatics (I was going to write 'fundamentalists', as if to whitewash the problem of calling people fanatical but changed my mind), I hope language pundits are not in the same league. The upset might be caused, by inference, by supposedly making fun of a duck that is 'cloomsy' or 'groompy'. It's only a duck and ducks can't speak! As mentioned in Chapter Ten, I have some northern antecedents; if not for them, I would not have had a chance to enter 'this sweet life'. One forebear owned three shops in Black-pool, one on the North Pier; they traded, amongst other things, in Irish linen that used to arrive in packet boats at the docks in Liverpool, usually accompanied by an escort of seagulls.

- In the *Daily Express* (26 November 2016), I was horrified to read an article, as follows: 'Thug beats student unconscious over her southern accent.' A 19-year-old girl in her first year at university, placing an order for chicken nuggets at a McDonald's branch, was suddenly stopped by a man who asked where she came from. The girl replied 'London', to which the man began swearing. She was called a 'f****** southerner'; he hated Londoners, calling them 'f****** tramps'. She was punched in the face, and 'the next thing I knew I was on the floor in a pool of blood'. Hence the injunction in Chapter Eleven to 'tread carefully', as accents are intrinsically personal.

- In Chapter Six, the journalist Giles Coren demonstrates his acerbic wit, but in an article in *The Times* (26 November 2016), Mr Coren writes so wittily about 'the boom in giant stupid great urban 4x4s owned by idiots' that I completely agree with him. He refers in his article to those 'appalling £75,000 all-terrain vehicles'. One of his cars is an old Land Rover Defender but he would 'no sooner bring it inside the M25 than I would walk a pig into a mosque'. He suggests that 'any sane person' must advocate that 'the owners of urban SUVs be forced to trade them in for smaller (ideally electric) vehicles and then be hung by their ankles from the nearest lamp post with "SATAN" carved on their chest with a Stanley knife'. He is a 'chip off the old block' too, as I seem to remember his father Alan Coren was a great wit, humorist, and journalist, an editor of *Punch* magazine, and team captain on the BBC's *Call My Bluff.* So hats off to Giles.

• On pp. 38–39 mention is made of Hull (and Grimsby). Just as northerners might joke about Bournemouth being fit only for white-haired invalids in bath chairs so Grimsby and Hull must have had some stick from southerners. Just how silly it is to make slighting observations about places (and by inference the people living there) really hit home when I discovered that the poet who wrote 'To His Coy Mistress', Andrew Marvell (1621–1678), was for twenty years the MP for Hull! As a young man I marvelled at Marvell complaining 'by the tide of Humber' whilst his love would be finding rubies along 'the Indian Ganges' side'. It was Marvell who wrote the marvellous lines, 'But at my back I always hear / Times wingèd chariot hurrying near…' Recently, I heard a bishop in the House of Lords praising another noble lord (I forget who). He said, 'A life of character and virtue, like a stick of Blackpool rock, has a message running all the way through it.' A life of character and virtue is to be measured equally – whether in Hull, Grimsby or Bournemouth; ditto Hampstead or Harrogate, Hackney or Hastings.

• Didn't you just know it! Once famously known as Britain's 'No. 1 Crap Town', Hull gets a mention in *Rough*

*Guides* – as one of the Top Ten cities to visit in 2017! Improbably, it's also been chosen as the UK City of Culture for 2017. Humberside is cool! (Two other 'born in Hull' notables are the anti-slavery crusader William Wilberforce and the superbly ironic poet Philip Larkin.)

- Mention is made *passim* of various MPs. There are scores of talented, hard-working members, and, as noted before, most mentions are just 'in passing'. Some notable (Conservative) MPs from the Home Affairs Select Committee are James Berry, Mr David Burrowes, Nusrat Ghani, Mr Ranil Jayawardena, and Tim Loughton. Iain Wright (Labour), chairman of the Business, Innovation and Skills Select Committee may have given the impression of being somewhat fresh-faced and young, up against the gnarled and experienced businessman Sir Philip Green but for his manly and bold questioning of the BHS tycoon he gained considerable kudos and stature. There are some 48 House of Commons select committees and about 34 House of Lords select committees. For anyone interested to learn more, *www. parliament.uk* is a treasure house.

- Just a quick mention of three more MPs. Jacob Rees-Mogg was reported on a Radio 4 programme as saying he likes to enjoy a relaxing hot bath late at night, after a long day in the House, but that he finds it tiresome to have to stand up in the bath when the National Anthem plays at closedown after midnight…This has the makings of a very good apocryphal story.

Neil Kinnock, Baron Kinnock PC (he's a member of the Privy Council, no less) refers to alma māters, with the 'a' in mater long (as in 'mate'); it's strange that 'pater' (father) is always pronounced with a long 'a'. To be fair, the 'long a' used in mater and pater are both 'long' but different (mater as in 'mart', pater as in 'fate'); no sign of the short 'a' as in 'cat'. (Lord Kinnock's alma mater is Cardiff University.)

I'd like to commend the ever mellifluous Kenneth Harry Clarke CH, QC (often known as Ken Clarke), connoisseur of brandy, ales and good cigars (alma mater: Gonville and Caius [pron. keys] College, Cambridge), a 'Big Beast' of the Conservative Party, for his pronunciation of 'desultory' (which means 'fitful' or jumping about from one thing to the next without much purpose or enthusiasm). He gets it right with 'DESS-ull-tree'. The Americans prefer 'dess-ul-TOR-EE', which sounds a bit like a species of fossilised or desiccated Tory. The Americans are really quite subtle, aren't they? They get FRUS-trated and we get frus-TRATE-(e)d.

• Whilst on the subject of MPs, many sit quietly during debates, saying very little other than a drowsy 'Hear! Hear!'. Others fit in the 'loquacious chatterbox' camp. Angus Robertson, for example, Deputy Leader of the Scottish National Party (SNP) is one (if always slightly dour), as is another Westminster SNP politician, Tasmina Ahmed-Sheikh, the Deputy Shadow Leader of the House in the House of Commons.

Sir Nicholas Soames, on a point of order, was obliged to apologise unreservedly to her on one occasion when he made 'woof, woof' sounds during one of her speeches. Sir Nicholas explained he thought she had been 'snapping at the heels' of the Foreign Secretary, Boris Johnson) in her speech, and the woofing sounds were merely 'a friendly canine salute'. Jim Shannon of the Democratic Unionist Party (DUP) is up on his feet a fair bit too.

- On page 57 I state my preference for county word-endings/suffixes (-shire) to be pronounced '-shur', e.g. Victoria Dar-bee-shurr (like the *shi* in *shirt*) rather than Victoria Dar-bee-shyre, noting it can also be '-sheer'. For once, I agree totally with EmmaSaying. She pronounces 'Derbyshire' exactly right, and it isn't 'Darby-sheer'. Of course, one talks of 'shires', the traditional Anglo-Saxon term for a division of land, and Shire horses (a breed of draught horse, or 'draft horse' in AmE).

- To add another term or word to 'stickler' and a person who likes 'gripes' in one form or another, author and journalist Peter Hitchens has described himself as a 'gloater'. As in, for example, a person who enjoys gloating over the discomfiture of 'remoaners'. Just time to say how easy it is to notice unusual, or even mischievous, pronunciations. Caroline Lucas of the Green Party spoke in a debate in the House about large 'pharma-cuticle companies'. You know, the ones with nails on. And in a session of *The Pledge*, Rachel Johnson said the reason why she knew the answer to a question was because she had learnt Latin at school. The phrase was 'ultra vires', acting beyond one's legal authority, and she pronounced it 'ultra veer-ess'. Now any Latin buff will tell you it's ultra VI-reez (although you can have both). EmmaSaying is not worth recommending on this (she makes a hash of it) but the online *Cambridge Dictionary* gets it perfectly.

• In any book about pronunciation one can only give a finite number of examples: to include every diffi-cult-to-pronounce word would be not only impossible but unprecedented (or 'unpresidented', as tweeted by Donald Trump), so the dedicated 'wordsmith' always has time go on making lists. There's lichen (pronounced liken); is it fun-jye, fun-guy or fun-gee for fungi; cho-rizo (in English, it's choh/REE/thoh, in AmE it's choh/REE/soh; not cho/RITZ/so the 'ch' sound as in 'char-coal' and not 'chorister'; but please don't take this as gospel as the Italians, Spanish, Portuguese, British and Americans can never agree on how to pronounce 'cho-rizo'; they only agree it tastes good), cardamom has a final 'm' not 'n', pancetta (panchetta), manzanilla, tor-tilla; obloquy, oeuvre, oligopsony (market with a small number of buyers); is it King Shar-le-main or Shar-le-mine for King Charlemagne ('Shar-le-mine' is a per-sonal preference of historian Simon Sebag Montefiore); how does one pronounce charivari (a mock serenade); a trompe doyle (heard on TV) or a *trompe l'œil* (a visual illusion in art, especially paintings)? *Note to Reader:* a few meanings/pronunciations of this small sample are omitted in order to pique your interest.

- If you like conjuring up the idea of ancient civilisations, I know I am not alone in having been seduced, if only marginally, by the word 'Byzantium', a word commonly used to refer to the Eastern Roman Empire whose capital in later times was Constantinople, now Istanbul. The former ancient Greek colony has an exotic ring, almost a halo, about it – like the magic conveyed by a single word in Shelley's sonnet: 'Ozymandius'.

But, how to pronounce 'Byzantine'? It seems there are at least *five* ways to say the word that refers either to the Byzantine Empire (and the Eastern Orthodox Church) or to things that are excessively complicated in detail (and possible devious). My first guide was EmmaSaying. She goes for 'Bi-zan-tyne' (the 'i' as in bicycle). Then, up popped Jeremy Paxman on *University Challenge* with 'Biz-an-teen' (the 'Biz' as in business). You could also write this as 'Biz-in-teen'. Just look at 'magazine' and 'mezzanine'; then compare with 'serpentine' and 'columbine'.

In summary, pronunciation can be a Byzantine quest on its own. I think an old saying serves well: 'It depends on which university you went to!' Often this comes down to: 'Blame the crusty old don (or give him thanks) who taught you *or* the open-necked professor in one of those arriviste red brick new universities.' Just to clear things up, the original *six* red brick universities are now part of the prestigious Russell Group. There are currently 24 Russell Group universities, originally 17. All have outstanding teaching, research and student facilities (and include Oxford, Cambridge, and the London School of Economics and Political Science (LSE)). This collection of high-ranking universities was formed by the universities themselves; they got their name because they always met in the Russell Hotel, London. So you see, things are not always as bad as they seem!

For a 'pronunciation twister', try this: 'The scolding scholar caused a schism when wielding scissors and a sceptre, and downing schnapps, though troubled in his schedule by sciatica.'

- As soon as one list is completed, along come more candidates. *Did you know* that Americans talk of an-CHO-vees but we prefer AN-cho-vees? Some say 'floral' to sound like floors, and some say floral to sound like laurel. Filipinos from the Philippines invariably talk about their 'press-i-dent', never a 'prez-i-dent'. And that item of hi-fi equipment, is it a wuffer or a woofer?

- Finally, on the same day (26 November 2016), Oliver Kamm, writing in his *Times* column (*The Pedant*) had some important things to say about English – accent and dialect. He cites Tom Wolfe's book, *The Kingdom of Speech* (see Chapter Nine), and refers to an earlier review he had written in which he called Wolfe's volume 'a celebration of ignorance and a vain, sneering, calumnious piece of fluff'. Critics say he 'hadn't really researched his subject properly'. In the same article, Kamm mentions the shadow education secretary, Angela Rayner MP, noting that she is from Stockport, and that her accent (like most of us) is 'specific to a geographical region'. Those who criticise her for not speaking more credibly or, say, with more grammatical correctness are, according to Kamm, 'ignorant of language'. He explains that 'Standard English is not an accent but a dialect'. All the non-standard dialects are equally valid. So, Standard English is not to be represented by one particular accent/dialect. The way someone speaks (their accent) cannot be equated to their intellect.

• Seventy years ago, the author of several English classics, Eric Partridge, said just the same thing in his *Pocket Guide to English Usage*. He quotes from H.W. Fowler: 'Dialect is [that] variety of a language which prevails in a district, with local peculiarities, and phrase...So dialects, therefore', he suggests, 'are languages *within* a language.' Partridge writes, 'It is to be hoped that dialect-speakers will not be shamed out of their words, phrases, and pronunciations by "cultured" visitors, by near-visioned teachers, by BBC "experts".' Furthermore, 'It is possible and indeed common to speak standard educated English with a regional accent.'

Standard English...began in the second half of the 14th century as the East Midland accent [used then at Oxbridge and in London]; it was a kind of compromise between the harshness of northern dialects and the 'drawling softness' of the southern. It gave no indication of where the speaker came from. Professor H.C.K. Wyld writes in his book, *The Growth of English*, how it is important to bear in mind that '…no form of language is, *in itself*, better than any other form. A dialect gains whatever place of superiority it enjoys solely from the estimation in which it is commonly held. It is natural that the language of the Court should come to be regarded as the most elegant and refined type of English…Of course, since this form of English is used in the conversation of the refined, the brilliant and the learned, it has become a better instrument for the expression of ideas than any other [variety] of speech now spoken.'

Professor Wyld continues: 'When we speak of Good English, or Standard English, or Pure English, as distinct from…Provincial English [the dialects proper], we must remember that there is nothing in the original nature of these…dialects which is in itself inferior or reprehensible, or contemptible.' Other dialects 'are in reality and apart from fashion and custom, quite as good as Standard English…considered simply as forms of language; but they have not the same place in general estimation, they have not been as highly cultivated ['… nor have they become so subtle and delicate', Partridge writes]…and they have not the same wide currency.' In any event, 'dialectical variety' is far more accepted today than ever before (as seen on TV!).

There are echoes of all the above in Oliver Kamm's article. He writes: '…standard English is not tied to a particular accent'. In his opinion, every scholarly linguist believes and knows that 'non-standard dialects of English are fully the equal in expressiveness, range and complexity of standard English...'. I find this truly enlightening. It means whether you write, 'She walks in beauty like the night / Of cloudless climes and starry skies', or 'As fair art thou, my bonie lass / So deep in luve am I' or 'That's a reet gradely lass on ower street', why, all are equally valid, equally expressive. All the more so if the non-standard dialect is the dialect of the speaker or writer, as people readily prefer their own accent or dialect; it's an indisputable part of personal heritage and identity – an identity within a group, a village, a county, a 'tribe', a geographical area.

Here, I would like to quote Oliver Kamm's really important message. It is that 'The value of knowing Standard English is not that it's "proper English" but simply that it's the most recognizable form of the language and is the dialect used in professional and public life.' He writes, moreover, that 'Prejudice against regional accents is no more rational or reputable than prejudice on grounds of ethnicity or sex.' It's too late now to change the title of this book so I hope the Reader will understand that the use of the word 'proper' in the subtitle of *The Mischievious Athalete* does not mean 'correct' English, in any way. I hope my duck will be appreciated, and whether he is 'grumpy' or 'groompy' will not matter one bit.

# GLOSSARY OF TERMS

(Including some not connected with
pronunciation, but added for good measure)

**Accent:** The way people pronounce words, depending on
which area, country or social group/class they come
from. Also the name for marks over letters to show
pronunciation, e.g. grave accent = à la mode, acute
accent = risqué. (Just in case *you don't know*, grave here
is pronounced like the first syllable in 'Ave [ah-vay]
Maria', the prayer to the Virgin Mary (['Hail Maria'])).

There's a good example of the way the Queen has
modified her accent over the years. A scientific study
of Christmas broadcasts to the Commonwealth over
several decades suggests 'the royal vowel sounds have
undergone a subtle evolution since the days when
coal was delivered to Buckingham Palace *in sex*'. (Neil
Tweedie, *Daily Telegraph*, 'How the Queen's English
has grown more like our own', 12 May 2006). (For

heaven's sake, Sharon Osbourne on *X Factor* says of a performance, 'Your'e so SAXY.' Too true vowel sounds are shifting.) There has been a move away from 'cut-glass to cockney [and mockney] as part of the blurring of class distinctions in Britain'. (*The Guardian*, 21 Dec 2000). The royals are having to adapt to changing times and long term social trends.

**Alliteration:** The repetition of an initial consonant sound in following words. Example: 'I *sl*ip, I *sl*ide, I *gl*oom, I *gl*ance' (from Tennyson's, *The Brook*. A more obvious example would be Peter Piper and his peck of pickled peppers. There's also Sally, the girl selling seashells on the seashore.

**Analogy:** Comparing A with B to draw attention to the similarity or comparability of two different things or ideas. Examples: 'Life is like a contest. Winner takes all and losers lose.' 'Spies and detectives function to hunt down criminals but in the body the police force is the immune system. Its job is to fight rogue cells.' 'Nurturing a child needs the same level of care and attention you would give to a treasured seed in your garden. Both need light, food, water and care if they are to survive.' And talking to strongly if they don't!

**Aphorism:** A short pithy saying used to express a general truth; maxim. E.g. 'Ars longa, vita brevis'. Originally coined by the Greek physician Hippocrates, 'Art is long, life is short'.

**Assonance:** The repetition of vowel sounds to make internal rhyming in phrases/sentences, more usual in verse than prose. 'How *o*dd of G*o*d/To ch*oo*se the J*e*ws.' 'How str*a*nge of m*a*n/To ch*a*nge the pl*a*n.' The assonance need not rhyme. Here's a proverb example: 'The e*a*rly b*i*rd catches the w*o*rm.'

**Bête noire:** A pet dislike, pet peeve; a person or thing that one particularly dislikes; bugbear. Something that annoys. Literally, 'black beast'. There's a fair number of bêtes noires in this book.

**Cliché:** An overworked expression past its sell-by date. Used so often it loses its novelty, original meaning or effectiveness. Said too often, so overworked and merely commonplace. 'As old as the hills', 'the writing on the wall', 'only time will tell'. You see, 'When it rains, it pours.'

**Cockney:** A cockney is native to London, especially the East End. Traditionally someone born within earshot of the bells of St Mary-le-Bow church. Cockneys are famous for their outspokenness and good humour, and for their rhyming slang (e.g. trouble and strife = wife; dog and bone = phone; china plate = mate; army and navy = gravy). The effect is to obscure the meaning of what is said or meant from outsiders. (Cockneys usually give as good as they get. The salt of the earth, many of 'em.)

**Dialect:** Regional or geographical speech patterns not considered to be the standard language dialect. A variation of a given language defined by locality or by reference to a group of people living within the given country.

**Double negative:** Two negatives used in the same sentence. That's two words of negation in a sentence when there should only be one. 'The hospital won't allow no more doctors as they say they already have enough.' 'Can't get no satisfaction', courtesy Rolling Stones. Also avoid words (some adverbs) treated as negatives (hardly, seldom, rarely, scarcely) and a negative in the same statement. 'He couldn't hardly believe his ears.' Cockneys like double negatives as in, 'You don't want none of 'em pronounciation guides – they don't do no good to no one.'

**Estuary English:** If you imagine a line with RP at one end and cockney at the other, Estuary English would sit in the middle. Generally, it's the name given to the modified form of regional accent(s) to be found around London, mainly in the southeast of England. 'No accent', says Paul Coggle in *Do you Speak Estuary?* (Bloomsbury Publishing, 1993), 'is intrinsically good or bad but it has to be recognised that the way we perceive accents does play a role in our attitude to others.' It was described by phonetician John C. Wells as 'Standard English spoken with the accent of the south-east of England.'

The main phonetic characteristics are described by John Wells as*: l-vocalization, glottalling, happ-Y-tensing, yod coalescence* but, unlike the cockney accent, without *h-dropping* or *th-fronting* (using labiodental fricatives). It's beyond the purpose (haha) of this book to explain in greater detail. For more, please search 'Estuary English PDF' from UCL Phonetics and Linguistics: 'What is Estuary English?'

**Euphemism:** Polite way of talking about usually taboo subjects by disguising them; often related to death, sex, bodily functions. Most common: 'He passed away' = died. Less common: 'Pointing Percy at the porcelain' = going for a pee; even less common, 'Tipping the velvet' (Victorian slang) = find that out for yourself! A long-running euphemism must be: 'A slept with B.'

The 30-year period of ruthless, near-war violence, murder, bombing, mayhem and knee-capping in Northern Ireland has a unique euphemism to describe it, so typically Irish. They call it 'The Troubles'!

**Faux pas:** A French word meaning 'false step', pronounced *fo pa*, plural written the same. A breach of etiquette or social blunder.

**FOOT–STRUT Split:** *See* Lexical sets.

**Glottal stop:** How do you perform one? You make a consonant, sound one, by a) closing the glottis, and b) obstructing airflow in your vocal tract, or making a 'plosive at the vocal folds', also known as 'glottalisation'. It's found not just in English but in many other languages around the world. Go 'uh-oh!' and you'll make a glottal stop. Or say 'Ga-wick' for Gatwick or 'muh'on' for mutton. It's like a momentary check on the airstream. The sound (or so I believe) goes through the nose as the airway is entirely blocked; the consonant is a 'stop'. It's a complicated subject in sociolinguistic studies (best not to go there...).

**Gripe:** When used in a pronunciation guide, it means to complain about something in a persistent, often irritating way, akin to bêtes noires.

**Homophone:** Words having the same pronunciation but usually quite different meanings/spellings. Examples: balmy and barmy; knew and new.

**Hyperbole:** naturally extravagant by exaggeration. Statements or claims not meant to be taken literally but used for effect or emphasis as in, 'I've defended millions of cases yet what have I got to show for it?' 'These guys are the best in the world.' 'I could look at her for ever.' (This means running the horse over a longer distance.) 'That horse has been crying out for a step up in trip.' The word comes from the Greek; hyper, over/above and beyond, the other part means 'I throw'. If it were ever possible, which I doubt, to give an example of a visible hyperbole made into a thing, a classic 'overthrow', think of Brad Pitt throwing the javelin in the film *Troy*. Of course he was portraying the god Achilles, so that's why the javelin or spear travelled at about 2000 mph for 500 yards. Later, when this was described, and put into words, the Greeks had a word for it: hyperbole (pron. hy-per-bŏl-lee).

**Hypercorrection:** Bending over backwards to try to (socially) fit in. People who hypercorrect think they know what the correct form of grammar is and attempt to 'bend the rules' to make it fit. 'I' and 'me' get confused so people imagine that if they say, 'The Queen invited my uncle and I for lunch', they've got it right but they haven't! The object in the sentence in grammar terms is 'my uncle and me' but it would be right to say, 'My uncle and I invited the Queen for lunch.'

**Idiolect:** This refers to the language of an individual as opposed to that of a group. It includes an individual's distinctive vocabulary, grammar and pronunciation, thus differing from a *dialect*, which refers to common linguistic characteristics that people in a defined group share.

**Infra dig:** Latin, *infra dignatem*. Beneath one's dignity. Demeaning.

**Jam:** The correct way to address the Queen, as in 'Ma'am', to rhyme with 'jam' (not Marm). Not to be confused with JAM families – those families just about managing (to make ends meet).

**Lexical sets:** Ways to list vowel sounds/pronunciation according to a keyword, invented by phonetician John Wells, including the TRAP–BATH split, the FOOT–STRUT split, GOAT, GOOSE, etc. 'Monday, Tuesday, Wednesday…' is a lexical set, don't you know.

**Malapropism (also malaprop, Dogberryism):** The mistaken use of a word, in place of one with a similar sound or pronunciation, often to humorous effect, such as the sixteenth chapel for the Sistine Chapel.

The eponymous Mrs Malaprop was a self-educated lady, a character created by Sheridan in his play, *The Rivals* (1775). Probably chosen from the word malapropos, meaning inappropriate, probably from the French, *mal à propos* (poorly placed). The word 'Dogberryism' comes from one, Dogberry, in Shakespeare's, *Much Ado About Nothing*, who had a similar habit. Examples: 'Don't upset the apple tart' (cart); 'Mr Trump is a huge suppository (repository) of information re Mexican migrants'; 'I thought it was water I saw in the desert but it was only a topical occlusion' (an optical illusion). Tony Hancock discussing famous actors, imagining he might be a famous actor too: 'There was Sir Laurence Olivier, Sir Ralph Richardson, and Sir John Gillgold…' (Gielgud).

TV presenter Kay Burley managed to make a marvellous new word at the time of Donald Trump's inauguration. She asked another reporter about the protests afterwards, saying [the protests were] '...not necessarily against Trump but against some of the messages he's been esparaging.' That sounds like a wholly ingenious conflation of espousing and disparaging. It's possible I misheard but I don't think so. Anyway, Kay did a great job that day, live presenting for hours.

Example of malapropism heard from a speaker at the Labour Party conference 2016, talking about members furious for being barred from voting in their leadership election, if a party member for less than six months. 'Comrades there's lots of court cases comin'. I think we're gonna be involved in a lot of legislation.' [litigation]

**Metaphor:** Whereas a simile compares two things, a metaphor does not use 'like' or 'as' or similar words but mentions two things, making an analogy (for rhetorical effect) between two things, suggesting a similarity that is not literally meant. Good old John Falstaff uses one in *The Merry Wives of Windsor* when he says to Pistol, 'Why then the world's my oyster.' 'The apple of his eye', 'On the battlefield he was a lion', 'Perfection is a first growth Bordeaux' are three further examples.

A mixed metaphor is using two or more metaphors together, usually with an illogical or ridiculous meaning. 'They've put all their eggs in one basket and it's misfired.' (Sky football pundit); 'A rolling stone is worth two in the bush'; 'How would you feel if I was sitting in your shoes?'

**Mockney:** Even George Osborne has tried it. A mockney speaker (usually middle or upper-middle class background) attempts to lower his (perceived) socio-economic class by 'dialect adoption'; imitating a cockney or working-class person with accent or speech/vocabulary patterns, usually *without* any non-standard forms such as double negatives (*see* double negative) or 'negative concord', e.g. A man asking employer for a job: 'You don't know no one as don't want nobody to do no job, do you?' To see George Osborne trying a mockney accent: see https://youtube.com/watch?v=Y1mbxFsp2x0.

**Mondegreen:** A misheard word or phrase, usually in song lyrics or poems. The hearer interprets the words incorrectly but it still makes apparent sense. The Beatles, 'Lucy in the Sky with Diamonds': 'The girl with kaleidoscope eyes' misheard as 'The girl with colitis goes by.' Or from Creedence Clearwater Revival, 'There's a bad moon on the rise' misheard as 'There's a bathroom on the right.' The linguists will tell you this is a result of a 'near-homophony'. For anyone who wants to look up obscure terms, there is also something called an 'eggcorn' (only for *really* dedicated word researchers).

Also obscure is a 'mumpsimus', which means someone who keeps repeating a habit, word, or mispronunciation even when knowing it's incorrect – and having been told so beforehand. (One often hears 'A hare's breath' as opposed to 'A hair's breadth'.)

Mondegreen's origin is from writer Sylvia Wright, who heard a Scottish ballad with the words, 'They hae slay the Earl of Murray, and Lady Mondegreen' but later she discovered the words were, '…and laid him on the green'.

**Neologism:** Coining a new word, either by reinventing a use of an existing word, a new meaning for an existing word, or something altogether new. Examples: spam, troll, staycation, digital detox, describing something as 'sick' = very good. When a neologism is accepted into the mainstream language, it's a neologism no more, e.g. 'to Google'.

Foreign Secretary Boris Johnson makes them up as he goes along, together with amusing if not startling ideas. In his 2016 speech to the Conservative party conference, he suggested that Jeremy Corbyn's idea to send Trident submarines to sea 'without nukes' was turning the service 'into a glorified military cāpon' [a castrated domestic cock fattened for eating] and as for Brexit doom-mongers, they were mere 'gloomadon poppers'. London 'acquired a deserved reputation as the greatest city on earth, a great jiving funkapolitan melting-pot…'

I'm sure 'double screen' is a neologism. People who 'double screen' too much are on their phones/laptops *and* watching TV. A new form of selfie is posting a 'belfie' on Instagram, which is a bum/butt selfie.

I blame Kim Kardashian for this, or those sitting on photocopiers.

'Snowflake' students are uni students who have to be warned in advance of lecture material that may possibly upset them. So theology students studying the life of Jesus need to be told that viewing 'Crucifixion scenes' might pose a threat to their well-being.

Two popular words in 2017 are 'post-truth', to mean a situation 'in which objective facts are less influential than appeals to emotion' (think Brexit and Trump); and the Danish word, *hygge* (pron. 'HUE-gah', meaning creating a warm, comforting, family atmosphere with candles, oversize scarves, and sitting round a table feeling ultra cosy.

**Onomatopoeia:** Words that sound very much like their intended meaning, the noise or action designated, or imitative of the sound of the noise or action intended. (This seems a laborious definition to me. Of course I wrote it.) Examples: hiss, cuckoo, meow.

**Orthography:** The accepted or 'correct' way of writing words and spelling them, including punctuation.

**Oxymoron:** An oxymoron is a figure of speech with contradictory terms or meanings: *An honest lawyer, the living dead, controlled chaos.* When I was trying to think up some new ones, an announcement was suddenly made on the TV – I'm sure I heard one. It was that the new shadow *culture* secretary was to be Tom Watson!

**Palindrome:** A word or phrase (adj. palindromic) that reads the same backward or forwards, such as eye, kayak, noon, racecar, radar, 'Madam I'm Adam', stressed desserts, etc.

**Plosive:** You sound a consonant such as 'p', 'b' or 't', and as you do this, the passage of air is completely blocked (bad luck). The 'block' may be between lips, tongue and teeth or tongue and palate. Related terms are bi-labial plosive, dental plosive and uvular plosive. Hence, this is not the place for further elaboration.

**Pun:** A humorous play on words, also called paronomasia. Puns have a long history in many human groups and cultures. Puns exploit ambiguities and innuendoes; this example from Thomas Hood:

> 'Ben Battle was a soldier bold,
> And used to war's alarms:
> But a cannonball took off his legs
> So he laid down his arms.'

Spanish ladies are said to be fond of punning. A young Spanish lady was once playing a piano in the presence of an English gentleman but did not sing to accompany her playing. On being asked to sing she replied, 'Mister, Yo no puedo *cantar*, pero puedo *encantar*.' 'I cannot sing, but I can *enchant*.'

A don met a porter crossing a quad with a hare under his arm, perhaps poached from Port Meadow in

Oxford. 'Prithee friend,' he said, 'is that thy own *hare*, or a *wig*?' This anecdote is said to be Charles Lamb's, discussing a premise 'that the worse puns are the best'. Puns are a bit like 'in-jokes'. They may be very funny, absurd or dreary. They are said to amuse dry old dons indefinitely.

**Received Pronunciation (RP):** An endangered species of 'prestige' English accent spoken by about 2-3 per cent of the population, predominantly southern.

**Simile:** A 'figure of speech' comparing one thing with another. Similes use 'connecting words' such as *like* or *as* to make the point. Mr Bean is 'as daft as a brush'. 'O My Luve's like,' wrote Robbie Burns, 'a red, red rose.' 'As mad as a hatter,' etc.

**Spoonerism:** The man responsible for (very) funny errors in speech was the Reverend William Archibald Spooner, 1844–1930. An albino with poor eyesight, and an overactive intellect that simply raced ahead of his tongue, this amiable character, who studied at New College, Oxford as a student and liked it so much he remained there as a lecturer for almost 60 years, donated to the world his extraordinary gift of mixing up sounds when 'pronouncing' on various subjects, an affliction he was seemingly powerless to prevent. These became known as 'spoonerisms', and here are five of his best (there's little doubt some were made up by Oxford students):

- Describing 'a well-oiled bicycle' as 'a well-boiled icicle'.
- To a bemused student, 'You have tasted a whole worm', instead of wasted a whole term. In full, this is said to have been: 'Sir, you have tasted two whole worms; you have hissed all my mystery lectures and have been caught fighting a liar in the quad; you will leave Oxford by the next town drain.'
- When making a speech to Queen Victoria: 'I have in my bosom a half-warmed fish' when he meant to say, 'I have in my bosom a half-formed wish.'
- Visiting another college, he asked, 'Is the bean dizzy?' for 'Is the dean busy?'
- When proposing a toast to our dear old Queen, the words came out as, 'To our queer old dean'.

**Standard English:** Standard RP pronunciation usually taught to non-native speakers as the best way to speak or pronounce English. Generally accepted as standard and used by most dictionaries published in the UK; 'eaten into' in some ways by EE (Estuary English).

**Stress:** The moronically challenged will suggest this is what happens to you when robbers point a gun and make off with £10m in jewellery. Here, it's the emphasis given in a word to a syllable(s), and may involve other linguistic terms such as pitch, duration or volume. Example = To conFER with someone at a CONference.

**Syllable:** This one is easier. The smallest unit of speech, may be a single vowel or a vowel and one or more consonants. Words of one syllable are monosyllables: 'cat', 'balls fell from his lap' has five syllables. Polysyllabic words that commonly cause difficulty in pronunciation are usually words of four or more syllables, such as: indubitably, Australopithecine, personification, trichomoniasis.

**th-fronting:** This is pronouncing 'th' as either 'f' or 'v', usually in cockney and Estuary English. 'Think' becomes 'fink' and 'bathe' becomes 'bave', for example. (For linguists, it involves *labiodental, and dental fricatives*.) If you are none the wiser, neither am I, very much. Think of a sound made by air passing somewhere between glottis (please look up glottis if not sure what it is) and lips, and a consonant formed by the lower lip touching the upper teeth. A good example of th-fronting must be: 'I fink, therefore I am.' René Descartes also said, *'Dubito, ergo cogito, ergo sum'* – for all you doubters out there. 'I doubt, therefore I *fink*, therefore I am.'

**TRAP–BATH split:** The simplest explanation? Imagine falling through a *trap*door into a *bath*. In some parts of the country, such as the north and midlands, a person will use the short 'a' vowel for both words but in other parts of the country, mainly in the south and east, people will use a short 'a' in *trap* but a long 'a' in *bath*. Hence the Trap–Bath split. *See also* Lexical sets.

**Trope:** A word employed by authors and journalistic commentators to suggest familiar, recurring literary and rhetorical devices, clichés, ideas, motifs, etc. Often used for effect, as in to sound educated. Usually implies a shift from literal to non-literal meaning. A 'personification trope' gives human attributes to non-human things, such as, 'The flowers embraced the sunshine, nodding their heads to this daily deity.' Hyperbole uses the trope of exaggeration: 'He's been here since the dawn of time.' An ironic trope: 'Your glossary of terms makes everything as clear as a blind man reading an encyclopaedia backwards whilst upside down in the bath.'

If that is not any clearer, please start again at the beginning!

# NOTES AND REFERENCES

## Introduction

1. https://en.wikipedia.org/wiki/Solecism

2. *The Times*, 26 July 2016

3. Ibid.

4. https://youtube.com/watch?v=bsjezTYrdE4

5. http://youtube.com/watch?v=QYx7caHqo84

6. https://youtube.com/#/watch?v.Pa1vXovXn-M

7. International Phonetic Association, *Handbook* (Cambridge: CUP, 1999)

8. https://en.wikipedia.org/wiki/International _Phonetic_ Alphabet

9. MacMahon, Michael K.C. (1996), 'Phonetic Notation' in P.T. Daniels and W. Bright (eds), *The World's Writing Systems.* (New York: Oxford University Press), pp. 821–46

10. *Drop Your Foreign Accent: Engelsche Uitspraakoefenignen* (Haarlem: H.D. Tjeenk Willink & Zoon, 1987–2), pp. 14–16

## Chapter 1

1. https://youtube.com/watch?v=uMJVAMD7axg

## Chapter 2

1. http://www.princeofwales.gov.uk/for-children/write-a-letter

2. https://www.ofcom.org.uk/research-and-data/tv-radio-and-on-demand/tv-research/offensive-language-2016

3. *The Times,* 25 July 2016

4. *The Times*, 9 December 2015

5. https://youtube.com/watch?v=jhninL_G3Fg

6. http://www.whichenglish.com/british-to-American-english?BEtoAE_A.html

## Chapter 3

1. Kingsley Amis, *The King's English: A Guide to Modern Usage* (London: HarperCollins, 1997)

2. John Betjeman, *The Best Loved Poems of John Betjeman* (London: John Murray, 2006)

## Chapter 4

1. http://www.bbc.co.uk/programmes/b01p6ryx

2. John Humphreys, *Lost for Words* (London: Hodder & Stoughton, 2004)

## Chapter 5

1. www.websudoku.com

## Chapter 6

1. *The Times* (Comment), 24 September 2016

2. *Daily Telegraph*, 14 August 2016

3. https://www.youtube.com/watch?v=KjTkkxzoyjE

4. *Daily Mail*, 2 September 2016

5. Hayley Dixon (17 March 2013), *Catholic Church is 'irredeemably corrupt'*, David Starkey claims (retrieved 8 September 2016), telegraph.co.uk

6. Stuart MacDonald (26 April 2009), *Call for David Starkey to say 'sorry' to Scotland*, (retrieved 7 October 2016), timesonline.co.uk

7. *David Starkey: Alex Salmond is a 'Caledonian Hitler'*, (retrieved 7 October 2016), telegraph.co.uk, 19 April 2013

8. *The Times* Register, 18 August 2016

9. 'Gregg Wallace: the bald, fat thug on MasterChef', in *iVillage* by Kyla Manenti (21 Jan 2011)

## Chapter 7

1. Story related by Simon Hoggart, the *Guardian*, 4 June 2001

2. Sky News presenter, Jeremy Thompson, 29 August 2016

## Chapter 9

1. *TMS, Times Diary*, 19 August 2016

2. https://youtube.com/watch?v=Q5MtlR1I20M

3. https://youtube.com/watch?v=w9BitscxBZc

4. Tom Wolfe, *The Kingdom of Speech* (London: Jonathan Cape, 2016)

## Chapter 10

1. Laurence Urdang, *Names & Nicknames of Places and Things* (London: Grafton), p. 146

2. Ibid., p. 278

3. *Daily Express*, 29 April 2015

## Chapter 11

1. From *The Collected Works* of W.B. Yeats

## Chapter 12

1. Joseph Conrad, *Heart of Darkness* (Penguin Classics, 2007). Originally published 1899

2. David Rosewarne, 'Estuary English' in *Times Educational Supplement*, 19 October 1984

3. *The Observer*, 27 June 1999

4. Turner, Lynn & West, Richard 2010, 'Communication Accommodation Theory, in *Introducing Communication Theory: Analysis and Application*, 4th edn (New York, NY: McGraw-Hill)

5. Giles, Howard; Coupland, Joustine; Coupland, N. 'Accommodation Theory Communication: Communication, Context, and Consequence', in

Giles, H. Coupland J. & Coupland N., *Contexts of Accommodation* (New York, NY: CUP, 1991)

6.  *University of Oxford Undergraduate Prospectus 2011*, University of Oxford, retrieved 3 September 2016

7.  https://en.wikipedia.org/wiki/John_C._Wells

8.  J.C. Wells, (1982) *Accents of English I: An Introduction.* (Cambridge: CUP), pp. 133–5 & 232

9.  *Evening Standard,* 8 September 2016

# Postscript

1.  Cole Moreton, 'Archbishop of Canterbury: "You have no future in the Church."' *Sunday Telegraph*, 11 November 2012

2.  From an English hymn by William Cowper, written in 1773

3.  https://youtube.com/watch?v=jepOx5AIVyY

4.  https://youtube.com/watch?v=FS4v5Ir1HEc

5.  Tom Utley article, *Daily Mail*, 2 September 2016

6.  https://youtube.com/watch?vGIvRMErZFr0

7.  https://youtube.com/watch?v.=ROM5

# SELECT BIBLIOGRAPHY

Kingsley Amis, *The King's English* (Penguin Modern Classics, 2011)

Jeremy Butterfield, *Fowler's Dictionary of Modern English Usage* (Oxford University Press, 2015)

David Crystal, *The Cambridge Encyclopedia of the English Language* (Cambridge: CUP, 2003, 2nd edn)

David Crystal, *The Stories of English* (Penguin Books, 2004)

David Crystal, *You Say Potato. A book about accents* (Macmillan, 2014)

Dr Johnson, *A Dictionary of the English Language* (1755)

Samuel Johnson, *Dr Johnson's Dictionary* (Penguin Classics, 2005)

Daniel Jones, *English Pronouncing Dictionary* (Dent, 1917)

Daniel Jones (Peter Roach, Jane Setter, John Esling, eds), *Cambridge English Pronouncing Dictionary* (Cambridge: CUP, 2011, 18th edn)

Patrick Kidd, *Diary at 50* (Times Books, London 2016). Extracts from TMS, *The Times Diary*. (Good source for apocryphal stories)

Tom MacArthur, *The Oxford Companion to the English Language* (Oxford University Press, 1996)

Robert McCrum, William Cran, Robert MacNeil, *The Story of English* (London: Faber and Faber, 2011)

Matthew Parris, *Scorn: The Wittiest and Wickedest Insults in Human History* (Profile Books, 2016)

Eric Partridge, *Pocket Guide to English Usage: A Guide to Good English* (Penguin Books, 2001). This edition revised by Janet Whitcut. Originally published in the UK by Hamish Hamilton. (A classic; a must for the buy/wish list. Also published as *Usage and Abusage*)

Lonely Planet, *British Language & Culture* (Lonely Planet, 2013)

John C. Wells, *Accents of English I: An Introduction* (Cambridge, New York: CUP, 1982)

John C. Wells, *Longman Pronunciation Dictionary* (Longman, 2008, 3rd edn)

# INDEX

*Reader's Note*

Pronunciation of particular words that are discussed in the text are *italicised*. Those that are discussed for meaning or comment are enclosed in quote marks. Page numbers followed by g refer to entries in the Glossary.

**A**

a, pronunciation of 100–2, 167–8
Abbott, Diane 90
abbreviations, use of 43
*absurd* 58
açai 97
accents 193g
accents *(general)* 122–4, 163, 173, 181–3
    see also specific accents, e.g. Scottish accent
*acknowledged* 4
addressing people 33–9
*adherents* 50
*advertisement* 53

*aesthetically* 78–9
'affidavit' 105
*Afghanistan* 29
*afternoon* 7
*again* 114
*against* 72
Ahmad, Lord 13
Ahmed-Sheikh, Tasmina 185
*aircraft* 39
alliteration 194g
alma maters 158–9
*almond* 125
'alright'/'all right' 166
*always* 66
*amateur* 68
*ambulances* 89–90

American pronunciation
15–16, 53–5, 66, 71,
75, 116–17, 172, 185,
189
American words for
English ones 53, 54,
139–41, 165
Amis, Kingsley 66
analogy 194g
*anchovies* 189
*Anglo Saxon Chronicle* 173
*Anthony* 172
anti-Semitism 75
*anything* 63
aphorism 194g
'Apocrypha' 105
'apocryphal' 105
*appreciate* 51
Aramaic 173–4
Archbishops, addressing 34
*ask* 103
*asphalt* 20
assonance 195g
*assume* 49
*asthma* 53
*astronomical* 73
*athlete* 55
*Audley* 78
*Australia* 148
Australian accent 158
*awry* 71

**B**
Baker, Danny 68
Balls, Ed 90
Barnes, William 18, 137–8
*basically* 109
*bath* 7, 64, 99–100, 163,
169, 208g
bath set 152
Bavin, Chris 95–6
BBC *see* newsreaders;
weather forecasters
BBC English 148
*Beaufoy* 62
*because* 58
*before* 44
'belfie' 203–4g
*Belvoir* 59
Bercow, John 13
*Berkeley* 16
bête noire 195g
Betjeman, John 66, 149
*Bicester* 59
*bike* 56
Black Londoner accent 124
black spider memos 33–5
Blackpool 131–3
Blair, Tony 9, 14, 29, 32
*bobbling* 131
*bombing* 72
Bone, Peter 109
*bookies* 5
'booty' 156
Bragg, Melvyn 145–6

Brand, Russell 145
*Brexit* 14, 54
*brioche* 97
Brown, Gordon 15, 17
Bruce, Fiona 40
Brummie accent 18, 122
*Bucket, Hyacinth* 27
Bucket, Hyacinth 49,
    111–12, 165
*burglar* 78
Burley, Kay 39–40, 200–1g
Burnham, Andy 31, 33, 34
Burns, Robbie 93–4
*bury* 91
*but* 31, 48
'bye now' 167
*Byzantine* 188

## C

*Caius* 9
Camden, William 172
Cameron, David 9, 51
Campbell, Glenn 7
'can't be doing with it'
    111–12
Canterbury, Archbishop of
    *see* Welby, Justin
*cappuccino* 24
*cardamom* 187
*carpe diem* 169
Carr, Jimmy 42
Carrington, Lord 14
Chamberlain, Bishop

Nicholas 156
*Charlemagne* 187
Charles, Prince of Wales
    33–5
*Charlotte* 87
*chassis* 16
Chequers 122
Chevening House 122
Chilcot Report 32
chimpanzee vocalization
    174
*chorizo* 187
*chuckle* 5
Churchill, Winston 105–6
*chutzpah* 110
*Cillit* 69
Clarke, Kenneth Harry
    185
clichés 41, 195g
*clumsy duck* 6
Coaker, Vernon 17
*Cockburn* 59, 126
Cockneys 56–7, 68, 124,
    144, 195g
cod fish accents 123–4
Coe, Lord 13
Coggle, Paul: *Do you Speak
    Estuary?* 196g
*cognoscenti* 168–9
*colonel* 108
Colvile, Oliver 152
*come* 91
*communal* 19

Communication Accommodation Theory (CAT) 146–7
*conference* 66
*congratulations* 16
Conservative English *see* Received Pronunciation
consonants, dropped 31–2
*constable* 66
*constituency* 50
*consumer* 50
*consuming* 51
*consummate* 49
Contemporary English *see* Received Pronunciation
*contention* 4
*controversy* 19
Cooke, Alistaire 50
'*Cooler, Faster, More Expensive: Return of the Sloane Ranger*' 37
Cooper, Tommy 84
Corbyn, Jeremy 48, 51, 89–90, 122
Coren, Alan 183
Coren, Giles 87–8, 182–3
Coren Mitchell, Victoria 87
Cormack, Patrick Thomas 39
Cornish accent 123–4
Cornwall 121
*cost* 94, 148

*Costa Rica* 76
'costermonger' 95–6
*costermonger* 96
*coup d'état* 42
*coupon* 78
*Coutts* 23
Cowell, Simon 48
Cox, Professor Brian 51
crafting on TV 82–4, 116–17
*crass* 14
Critchley, William xi–xii
    family 131–3, 181–2
Croxall, Martine 40
*crude* 20
*crudités* 97
Crystal, David 170
*Cumberbatch, Benedict* 24

**D**

*Daily Telegraph* 43
Daly, Tess 82
*Darbyshire, Victoria* 186
*Dash* 77
Davis, David 122
Davis, Evan 39
*debacle* 109
*debate* 96
'*Debrett's Peerage & Baronetage*' 37
*decathlon* 114
*December* 58
déclassé 79

*defensive* 96
deferably, use of 41
*delivery* 45
*democracy* 45
Demosthenes 3
Denning, Lord 3, 10
*deportation* 45
*derby* 16
Desai, Lord 13
*desultory* 185
*deterrent* 45
*detour* 45
diagraphs 22
dialects 190–1, 196g
    *see mainly* accents
*dictators* 15–16
*did you* 109
'Did you know' 126
'diddly-squat' 88
Dimbleby, David 98–9
Dinenage, Fred 17
divergence 146–7
*diversion* 117
*divorce* 96
Dogberryism 200g
*Doncaster* 99
*Donne* 61
'Don't you know' 126
Dorset vernacular 137–8
double negatives 56, 103, 196g
'double screen' 203g
Dowd, Peter 109

Doyle, Dean 157
Doyle, Mrs 151
dress codes 170–1
Duchy Estate 134–5
dumbing down 42–3
*duty* 54
*duvets* 50
Dyke, Greg 12, 145–6
dysrhotic r 115–16

**E**
e, pronunciation of 43–5
Eagle, Angela 31
*eat* 125
*Edgbaston* 99
Edwards, Huw 7
eggcorn 202g
'Eisteddfod' 106
*either* 53
*eleven* 45
Ellinas, Maria 48
elocution 2–3
*Elysium* 79
EmmaSaying 23–4, 65, 92, 109, 117, 125, 169, 172, 186, 187, 188
English alphabet 159
English pronunciation poem 175–80
Ennis, Jessica 49
*enthusiastic* 51
*entrepreneurs* 68
*envelope* 93

*er* 66
*erm* 66
*escalate* 55
Esler, Gavin 7
'esparaging' 201g
'espresso' 106
Estuary English 3, 32,
    48, 81, 143–4, 151–2,
    196–7g
*et cetera* 121–2
Eton College 44, 158–9
euphemism 197g
*Europe* 14
*event* 44
*executive* 50, 121
*exude* 52

## F

Falconer, Charlie 15
Falk, Peter (as Lieutenant
    Colombo) 36
Falstaff, John 201g
Farron, Tim 15
faux pas 197g
Fearnley-Whittingstall,
    Hugh 65
Fettes College 14
Field, Frank 44
Fiennes, Ralph 11
Filipinos 189
*film* 63
*floral* 189
Floyd, Keith 149

FOOT–STRUT split 168,
    200g
*forecast* 7–8
*forehead* 65
Foreign Secretary's
    residence 122
foreign words 2, 96–8
*Fotheringay* 62
Fowler's *Modern English
    Pronunciation* 111, 190
Fox, Liam 122
*fragile* 15
*France* 40
*frustrated* 185
*fungi* 187

## G

*gala* 28
*garage* 126
Garden Bridge 152–3
gender 80–2
Geordie accent 123
*gerrymandering* 109, 110
Gielgud, John 11
Giles, Howard 146–7
'Ginger' 36
*glacier* 139
*Glasgow* 11
'gloater' 186
glossolalia 158, 160
glottal stop 121, 145, 168,
    197–8g
*going to* 54–5

*goose bumps* 65
*gooseberries* 65
*Gospel of Mark, The* 94
*graph* 64
*grass* 100
*grave* 193g
Grayling, A.C. 120
Green, Sir Philip 35, 44, 52, 184
gripe 198g
*grumpy duck* 5

**H**
h, pronunciation of 45–6, 144
*had to* 76
*half-* 101–2
*hamster* 117
Hancock, Tony 200g
*handkerchief* 111
*handsome* 111
Harrison, Rex 46
*health* 58
*hearth* 100
Heath, Ted 29
*herbs* 16, 172
Hiddleston, Tom 11
high rising terminal 158
Highlands land ownership 134–5
Hill, Jane 40
Hillier, Meg 10–11
*history* 114

Hitchens, Peter 186
Hitchiner, Rev Sally 155
Holmes, Eamonn 7
*Holyrood* 115
Home Counties 130
*homicide* 58
homophone 198g
*horses* 81–2
Hughes, John (Bishop of Kensington) 158
Hull 183–4
*human* 15
Humphrys, John 7, 76
Husain, Mishal 39
*hybrid* 68
'*hygge*' 204g
hyperbole 198–9g, 208g
hypercorrection 47, 129, 147, 199g
hypolingual r 115–16

**I**
idiolect 199g
*impromptu* 117
Indian accent 73
infra dig 199g
Inns of Court 159
*insulin* 21
International Phonetic Alphabet 24–5
*involved* 58
*Iraq* 53
Irish accent 7, 22, 63, 78

Irish names 151
Irish Republic accent 122
Irons, Jeremy 84
Islam, Faisal 54
'isn't it?' 129
*Isphahaan* 157
*Israeli* 72
*issue* 51, 92
*isthmus* 72

**J**
Jafaican accent 124
jam *see* Ma'am
Jamaican accent 6–7
Jenkins, Roy 115–16
'Jock' 36
Johnson, Boris 66, 76,
   88–9, 122, 186, 203g
Johnson, Dr 6
Johnson, Rachel 75–6,
   186–7

**K**
Kamm, Oliver 152–3,
   189–90, 191–2
*karaoke* 123
Kardashian, Kim 204g
Kay, Peter 81
Kay, Vernon 85, 123
*Kenya* 148
Keynes, John 77–8
*Keynes* 61
Khan, Sadiq 32

*kilograms* 20
*kilometres* 20
Kim Jong-un 171
Kinnock, Neil 50, 185
Kipling, Rudyard 14
Kirkwood, Carol 8
Knightley, Keira 81
Kwarteng, Kwasi 12

**L**
l-vocalization 168
Lamb, Charles 36
*land* 148
languages of the world
   159–60
*Lascelles* 60
Latin abbreviations, use of
   42–3
latté 4
'lavatory'/'loo' 165
*Leicester* 59
Leonard, Kimberley 40
Leslie, Chris 74
*leverage* 52
Lewis, C.S. 149
lexical sets 200g
LGBT 155–6
*lichen* 187
*lieutenant* 36
'like' 75
linguistics 22–3, 152
Lisvane, Lord 91–2
'literally' 84

*little* 55–6
Liverpudlian accent 18, 173
*local* 8
London accent, South 124
London taxi drivers 56
long words 80
*longevity* 97
Lucas, Caroline 186
Lumley, Joanna 9, 152
Lutyens, Edward 20
*luxury* 54

**M**
*Ma'am* 28
McDonnell, John 51–2
McGovern, Steph 123
McGuinness, Joseph
    'Paddy' 81–2, 123
*machinations* 168
*Magdalen(e)* 59–60
mainstream English *see*
    Received Pronunciation
Mair, Eddie 7
Maitlis, Emily 40
malapropism 200–1g
*Mallorca* 28
*maniacal* 171
*manoeuvring* 112
'mardy' 163
*margarine* 28
*Marlborough* 125
Marvell, Andrew 183
'mash' 163

Mason, Chris 45
Mason, Paul 45
*masseuse* 68
*mater* 185
*May, Theresa* 40
May, Theresa 88
*me* for *my* 31–2
mealtime names 163
meanings of words,
    changing 156
*medal* 55
medical words 105
*medieval* 58
Meldrew, Victor 65
*mêlée* 21
Members of Parliament
    9–15, 17, 29, 30–1,
    38–9, 43, 44, 51–2, 74,
    89–90, 109–10, 184–5
Mercury, Freddie 156
metaphor 201g
*Michelle* 123
Middle Temple xi
Milliband, Ed 14, 31, 75
*Milliband, Ed* 44
Millican, Sarah 81
Mirren, Dame Helen 81
*mischievous* 19
*misled* 71–2
mispronounced words list
    103–10
    *see also specific words*
Mitchell, Andrew 43

Mitford, Nancy 164
mockney 3–4, 15, 145, 202g
mondegreen 202–3g
*Morrisons* 43, 125
*Moscow* 16
*Mountjoy* 62
mumpsimus 202g
Munch, Edvard 9
'*My Fair Lady*' 46
Myers, Dave 20
Myrie, Clive 96

**N**
*naan* 165
names 151
      pronunciation of
      59–61
'napkin' 163–4
*Nasser, President* 50
*Navratilova* 80
*negotiate* 92
Neil, Andrew 54
*neither* 53
neologism 203g
New Zealand accent 158
*Newcastle* 5
newsreaders 2, 6–7, 21, 32,
      39–40, 49, 57, 58, 123,
      170–1
Newton Dunn, Tom 150
*niches* 75
'nigga' 36
non-U speech 164–5

*none* 38
Northern accent 123, 181–3
Norton, Graham 46
*nuclear* 106
Nunes, Neil 7
*nutrient* 50

**O**
Oakeshott, Isabel 150
*Obama, Barack* 40
O'Brien, James 40
obviously, use of 41
Occam's razor 80
'*Official Sloane Ranger
      Handbook*' 37
*often* 111
'oligopsony' 187
Oliver, Neil 115
Olivier, Laurence 11
Omaar, Rageh 11–12
*one* 4
onomatopoeia 204g
'ordinance' 106–7
'ordnance' 107
*oregano* 16, 172
orthography 204g
Osborne, George 54, 202g
Osbourne, Sharon 194g
*-ough* 110
'outwith' 162
Oxford English *see*
      Received Pronunciation
oxymoron 204g

# P

Packham, Chris 58
*Pakistan* 29–30
Pakistani accent 73
palindrome 205g
*Pall Mall* 125
*pancetta* 187
*paprika* 172
*parliament* 91
'*Parliament*' (BBC) 9, 10
paronomasia 205–6g
Parris, Mathew 46
Partridge, Eric: *Pocket Guide to English Usage* 190
*party* 48
*passport* 64
Patel, Priti 29, 32
*pater* 185
Paterson, Niall 7
*patron* 21
Paxman, Jeremy 98, 188
pedantry 155
*penis* 24
*percolator* 55
*perhaps* 66
'perpetrator' 77–8
*Persepolis* 157
'persiflage' 168, 169–70
*pessimism* 53
'*Peter York's Hipster Handbook*' 37
*pharmaceutical* 186
phonemes 159–60

phonetics 24–6, 46
phonology 152, 159–60
*photos* 8
phrases, OK vs not so OK 166–7
*piano* 110
Pickles, Sir Eric Jack 74–5
Pidgen English 78
*pistachios* 64
Pitt, Brad 198–9g
*pitta* 76
*plants* 40
plausible 112
*plethora* 10
Plomley, Roy 74
plosive 205g
*plughole* 69
*police* 66
*pollution* 50
*post* 8
'post-truth' 204g
*potholes* 69
*pound* 8
*preferable* 19
*prelude* 43
Prescott, Lord 5–6
prime ministers 158–9
*privacy* 53
*problem* 65–6
*projects* 20
*pronunciation* 2
pronunciation, what it is 2–3

proper nouns
    pronunciation of
    59–61
    *see also* names
*prosciutto* 97
'prostrate/prostate' 107–8
*proven* 40
*psoriasis* 108–9
'pudding' 164
pun 205g
*pursue* 49–50
Putin, Vladimir 16

## Q

*quality* 80
Queen's speech 2, 193g
question tag 129
quilting 116–17
*quinoa* 97
Qur'an 73

## R

r, pronunciation of 115–16
race and colour on media
    12–13
Rae, Susan 7
Raworth, Sophie 40
Rayner, Angela 30, 50, 190
*really* 148
*rebel* 25
Received Pronunciation
    7, 49, 50, 54, 66, 81,
    105, 111, 115, 122,

143, 145, 147–9, 190,
    190–2, 206g
*recognise* 55, 121–2
*recover* 44
*redress* 114
Rees-Mogg, Jacob 11, 13,
    184
'reet gradely' 131–3, 137
*regime* 73
regional accents 6–9, 17–19
*regulator* 121
Reith, Lord 148
*reject* 45
*relegate* 19
*reneged* 58
'reoccur/recur' 108
*respect* 32
*respite* 71
*retain* 114
*retire/ment* 45
*reward* 45
*rhetoric/al* 17
rhotic r 115
Richardson, Ralph 11
'riding' 160–1
Rigby, Beth 31–2
Rivers, Joan 81
Robertson, Angus 185
Robinson, Anne 45
Romford Man 19–20, 56,
    68
*room* 65
*rose* 100–1

*rosemary* 172
Ross, Alan 164
Royal Family, addressing 35
Rushdie, Salman 10
Russell, Bertrand 119–20
Russell Group 189
Ryan, Katherine 81

**S**

s, pronunciation of 47–8
*saboteurs* 68
*salmon* 125
Salmond, Alex 93
*Sartre, Jean-Paul* 54
*says* 38
*scallop* 68
Schama, Simon 90
*schedule* 54, 126
*sclerosis* 109
*scone* 27, 94
Scotland 134
Scots, addressing 36
Scottish accent 4, 6–8, 20,
    22, 49, 56, 93–4, 115
Scottish names 150–1
Scouse accent 18–19, 124
        *see also* Liverpudlian
        accent
*Seamus* 61
*secretary* 121–2
*secure* 15
Select Committee
    Members 184

'serviette' 163–4
'settee' 162
*sewer* 15
shaft 39
Shakespeare, William 21,
    113, 145
*-shires* 57, 186
simile 206g
Simpson, Professor Steve
    123
Sir, addressing people as
    35–6
Skinner, Dennis 13
Sky News 40
slips of the tongue 109–10
*sloth* 169
Smith, Sheridan 81
'snowflake' students 204g
So... 58
Soames, Sir Nicholas 29,
    30, 51, 92, 105–6, 186
*soften* 111
solecism 3
*Solti* 110
*'South at Six'* (BBC) 17
speech 127–8
speech sounds 159–60
spelling differences with
    same pronunciation 110
'splendid' 152
Spooner, Rev William
    Archibald 206–7g
spoonerism 206–7g

sports presenters 55
squaddie 67
*squirrel* 108
*Sri Lanka* 29
Standard English 207g
    *see mainly* Received
    Pronunciation
Starkey, David 91, 92–3
'steatopygia' 108
Steele, Jane 40
Stein, Rick 64
'step up to the plate' 155
stock phrases 41
Stourton, Edward 12
*strafing* 75
strangers, addressing 35
*street* 48
stress 207g
*struggle* 47
Stuart, Jamie 94
*student* 47
*stupid* 103
Sturgeon, Nicola 115,
    133–4
*success* 131
Sudoku 84
*sue* 49
*Suez* 50
*suitcase* 50
*Sun* editor 150
*super* 49
*sure* 15
*swathe* 53

swearing 80–1, 82
syllable 208g

**T**
t, dropped 30–1
t, pronunciation of 48,
    55–6, 197–8g
'Taff' 36
taxi drivers in London 56
*tedious* 71
Teeside accent 123
teleshopping 82–4
th, pronunciation of 152,
    197g, 208g
Thames, River 143–4
Thatcher, Margaret 11
*theatre* 20
*thegns* 173
*them/those* 112–14
*think* 103
*thirteen* 57
Thompson, Louise 79–80
*thoroughbred* 63
*those/them* 112–14
*thyme* 172
'to be honest' 21, 41, 79,
    82, 90, 99, 103, 115
'to be honest' use of 41
*'Today'* (BBC) 12
'toilet' 165
Toksvig, Sandi 86
*tomatoes* 139
*toothbrush* 65

*tortoise* 17
TRAP–BATH split 167–8, 200g, 208g
*treatise* 3
Trenité, Gerard Nolst 25–6
    *The Chaos* 175–80
*trompe l'oeil* 187
trope 209g
'trump' 139–40
*tune* 82
Turnbull, Bill 89
*turquoise* 17
Tusk, Donald 89
TV presenters/programmes 42, 58, 79, 81, 82–4, 85–90, 91, 95, 98, 116–17, 130–1
    American 86–7
    *see also* newsreaders; weather forecasters
Tweedie, Neil 193g

**U**
u, pronunciation of 48–9
U speech 164–5
uk.gov web portal sites 42–3
*ultra vires* 186–7
*um* 66
Umunna, Chuka 10
undertones 112
Upper received Pronunciation 148

upspeak 158
Urban, Mark 75
Utley, Tom 92, 170

**V**
v, pronunciation of 73
*Van Gogh* 54
*vase* 16
Vaz, Keith 9–10
*vehicle* 15
*veneer* 68–9
*Venus de Milo* 45
vernacular, changing to 145–6
*via* 15
*victuals* 97
*Vosne* 162
vowels 5, 24–6, 65
    *see also specific vowels*

**W**
w, pronunciation of 73
w, used for r 115–16
Waitrose 27–8
Wallace, Greg 95–6
Walsh, Bradley 85
Wark, Kirsty 20
'wasn't it?' 130
Watson, Iain 7
Watson, Tom 204g
Watt, Nick 40–1
Wax, Ruby 81
'WC' 165

weather forecasters 8–9
'wee' 36
Wehn, Henning 88, 109
Welby, Justin (Archbishop of Canterbury) 158
Wells, John C. 149, 196–7g
Welsh accent 7, 50, 57, 122
Welsh names 150
*Wembley* 78
Westmacott, Sir Peter 16
*wh* 22
*whale* 22
'What do we own?' 126–7
Wilde, Oscar 139
Winchester r 115–16
wine knowledge and pronunciation 161–2
Winnick, David 52
Winslet, Kate 81
Winton, Dale 86
Wodehouse, P.G.: *Right Ho, Jeeves* 137

Wogan, Sir Terry 7
Wolfe, Tom: *The Kingdom of Speech* 127, 189–90
*world* 56
Worricker, Julian 57
Worsthorne, Sir Peregrine Gerard 11, 110
Wright, Iain 184
Wyld, Prof H.C.K.: *The Growth of English* 191

**Y**

*year* 56
*Yeats* 61
Yeats, W.B.: 'The Cloths of Heaven' 138
*yogurt* 54
York, Peter 37
Yorkshire accent 18
Young, Kirsty 7

**Z**

*z* 16
*zucchini* 24

www.ingramcontent.com/pod-product-compliance
Lightning Source LLC
Chambersburg PA
CBHW050112280326
41933CB00010B/1065